The Practitioner Inquiry Series

Marilyn Cochran-Smith and Susan L. Lytle, *SERIES EDITORS*

ADVISORY BOARD: Rebecca Barr, Judy Buchanan, Robert Fecho,
Sarah Freedman, Karen Gallas, Dixie Goswami, Andrew Gitlin, Peter Grimmett,
Roberta Logan, Sarah Michaels, Susan Noffke, Susan Florio-Ruane, Marsha Pincus,
Marty Rutherford, Lynne Strieb, Carol Tateshi, Polly Ulichny, Diane Waff, Ken Zeichner

Creating Democratic Classrooms:
The Struggle to Integrate Theory and Practice
LANDON E. BEYER, Editor

CREATING DEMOCRATIC CLASSROOMS

The Struggle to Integrate Theory and Practice

LANDON E. BEYER
Editor

Teachers College, Columbia University
New York and London

Published by Teachers College Press, 1234 Amsterdam Avenue, New York, NY 10027

Copyright © 1996 by Teachers College, Columbia University

Library of Congress Cataloging-in-Publication Data

Creating democratic classrooms : the struggle to integrate theory and
  practice / Landon E. Beyer, editor.
     p.   cm. — (The Practitioner inquiry series)
  Includes bibliographical references and index.
  ISBN 0-8077-3519-1 (cloth). — ISBN 0-8077-3518-3 (pbk.)
    1. Teachers—Training of—United States—Philosophy.   2. Critical
pedagogy—United States.   I. Beyer, Landon E., 1949–
II. Series.
LB1715.C72   1996
370.71—dc20   95-51170

ISBN 0-8077-3518-3   (paper)
ISBN 0-8077-3519-1   (cloth)

Printed on acid-free paper
Manufactured in the United States of America

03 02 01 00 99 98 97 96   8 7 6 5 4 3 2 1

To the progressive students and teachers with whom I have worked during the last 15 years, and to those I will teach and be taught by as we struggle to create a more educationally invigorating and socially just future.

Contents

Foreword ix

Acknowledgments xi

**1. Introduction:
The Meanings of Critical Teacher Preparation** 1

Landon E. Beyer

2. The Bumpy Bus Ride to the Democratic Classroom 27

Erin Roche

**3. Creating Space:
Moving from the Mandatory to the Worthwhile** 41

Ushma Shah

**4. The Rock House:
Barriers in Education and Their Demolition** 62

Joni Garlock

5. Building Bridges Toward Democracy 73

Noelle Hawk Jaddaoui

**6. Creating a Democratic Classroom:
Empowering Students Within and Outside School Walls** 87

Krista Sorensen

7.   **To Give My Students Wings**   **106**

     Katie Poduska

8.   **Vision, Vitality, and Values:**
     Advocating the Democratic Classroom   **127**

     Mary Cunat

9.   **Conclusions:**
     A Look Backward and the Road Ahead   **150**

     Landon E. Beyer

About the Contributors   **163**

Index   **165**

Foreword

This book is the first in a new series on Practitioner Inquiry that will include teacher research, action research, participatory research, and related
forms of inquiry in education by teachers, administrators, staff developers,
teacher educators, and others. Over the past decade, classroom teachers,
school and university collaborators, and other educators have been constructing a new set of challenging questions about the relationships of practice,
knowledge, policy, and power in the contemporary educational reform movement. These questions suggest an agenda for the future of practitioner inquiry as a movement and require a conceptually coherent program of pub-
lication. The new Practitioner Inquiry Series is designed to further the
national conversation in this area among the growing community of educators committed to this work. Based on a broad and inclusive conception of
practitioner inquiry, this new series will include both empirical and conceptual research and writing by school, university, and program-based teachers, administrators, and other practitioners. It will feature research about
the processes and outcomes of practitioner inquiry in professional development and teacher education, school-site projects that use practitioner research as a vehicle for school reorganization and curriculum development,
and local and state level policies that are implemented or assessed through
practitioner research.

*Creating Democratic Classrooms: The Struggle to Integrate Theory
and Practice* is based on the assumptions that education is a fundamentally
social and political endeavor, that it is sorely in need of revitalization along
more progressive lines, and that teachers who engage in critical practice can
play a central role in reinventing schools and schooling. Beyer's introductory and final sections frame the volume, a collection of essays written by
seven classroom teachers who have participated with Beyer in a teacher
education program designed to promote critical perspectives on current
educational practice and the development of alternative pedagogies. The
contributing authors vary in the extent of their teaching experience and teach
in a variety of school contexts, but share with Beyer the belief that the daily
life of classrooms is inextricably linked to social theory and social life. Each
essay includes classroom vignettes and other rich details of teachers and

students at work, interwoven with teachers' questions, dilemmas, and interpretive frameworks. Taken together, these essays provide multiple windows on critical practice that intentionally locate the issues of daily life in classrooms within a larger framework of education for democracy.

A major contribution of this book is its deep rootedness in teachers' own analyses of their ongoing efforts to engage children in meaningful dialogue—dialogue about problems of genuine significance for both immediate classroom life and the larger agenda of social justice to which they are connected. The book also speaks to the importance of inquiry-oriented teacher education programs across the professional lifespan that promote progressive visions of education animated by what Beyer calls "the politics of hope." Finally, this volume attests to the growing realization that teachers who engage in critical practice are strongly positioned to enrich and alter our understandings of teaching as a moral and political activity.

Marilyn Cochran-Smith and Susan L. Lytle
Series Editors

Acknowledgments

Several people were instrumental in getting this project off the ground, and in seeing it through to completion.

First, the authors included in this volume worked diligently not only on their individual contributions, but in helping and supporting each other; this was truly a communal project whose fruits must be shared by all.

Second, both Brian Ellerbeck and Carol Chambers Collins of Teachers College Press were supportive and encouraging from the beginning. I thank them for their cogent comments and suggestions, and for their thoughtfulness and good humor.

Third, a significant amount of work on this project was completed as part of my sabbatical leave during the 1992–93 academic year. For about half of that time I was pleased to be a resident of Friday Harbor Laboratories, Friday Harbor, Washington. During that time the staff and researchers at Friday Harbor were generous in providing library research assistance, access to relevant resources, and intellectual and moral support. They generally made my stay there a model of involvement. I am especially grateful to Dennis Willows, Director of Friday Harbor Labs. I appreciate his gracious assistance with this project, and admire his democratic orientation to the day to day activities of the lab itself and to the social life it engendered.

CREATING DEMOCRATIC CLASSROOMS

The Struggle to Integrate
Theory and Practice

ONE

Introduction:
The Meanings of
Critical Teacher Preparation

Landon E. Beyer

Like everything else, the domain of public schooling has a history and an undergirding set of assumptions and traditions. These are influential in shaping our understanding of the purposes of schools and the practices of teaching. Periodically these histories and assumptions have become the subject of reinterpretation and analysis, with resulting calls to reform educational institutions. We continue to be in a period of such reform as we near the close of this century—a time when significant changes in educational practices and orientations seem possible, in spite of the obstacles involved (Sarason, 1990). Such changes are only feasible, however, if educators remember the past and the assumptions by which we have been guided, if we develop alternative perspectives, principles, and strategies, and if we remember the contexts within which schools function.

Virtually from the beginning of the campaign to establish a system of public education in the United States, advocates have argued that schools are meritocratic institutions that function to expand individual opportunities and further the social good. These educational orientations were allied with a belief in progress that is one of the hallmarks of modernism and a faith in America as the land of opportunity. Influential spokespeople touted a system of education that would provide perhaps the primary avenue to political self-determination and levels of unprecedented material prosperity based on students' native abilities and their commitment to hard work, diligence, and perseverance.

These beliefs were bolstered by the more general assumption that we live in an open, accessible, fair society that offers political freedoms through a system of representative democracy, and opportunities for social mobility through a capitalist economy. Another element of this framework was provided by a commitment to individualism inherited from the classical liberal tradition (Bellah, Madsen, Sullivan, Swidler, & Tipton, 1985; Lukes, 1973). A world view was constructed according to which people are relatively isolated, perfectible, perpetually striving beings to be judged according to their native talents teamed with their individual commitment to a work ethic. Schools continue to be depicted as institutions devoted to fairness and equality of opportunity, and, hence, to providing the means to individual success and social prosperity. We can understand, thus, why school boards, administrators, teachers, and parents might come to regard schools as embodying ideas and activities that are necessary and frequently, in broad outline, beyond reproach—except when they have a negative impact on our daughters or sons or when they violate a set of values that we hold in especially high regard. Within these guiding assumptions and traditions, the basic question of what schools are *for* has often seemed naive, its answer self-evident.

This picture of schooling has helped foster the view that educational institutions are, and need to remain, separated from ideological disputes and divisive value conflicts. Teachers have been thought responsible for passing on those forms of knowledge that have "withstood the test of time" or otherwise constitute the basics, and inculcating in students those values, dispositions, and habits that provide a kind of cultural glue necessary for social life (Bennett, 1994; Bloom, 1987; Finn, 1991; Hirsch, 1987). An emphasis on what is true and/or socially necessary has provided the epistemological basis for excluding particular subjects, events, and interpretations, and has served to support the view of schools as non-ideological. When it is suggested that value-laden questions and conflicting perspectives ought to be a part of the school curriculum, a common response has been that the teacher might, at most, introduce such questions and perhaps note that they have given rise to differing points of view. It is far less common for normative disputes to be encouraged as a way of understanding a multiplicity of perspectives—with some exceptions, of course (see, for instance, Newman, 1970). The result is that much teaching and curriculum—perhaps best represented by the development of the textbook (Apple, 1987; Shannon, 1988)—has been focused on a middle-of-the-road, "strictly factual" pseudo-intellectualism that drains the lifeblood from issues over which considerable intellectual struggle has taken place. We have tended to sponsor a form of teaching and curriculum bounded by a tacit commitment to "official knowledge" of a sort that is hardly value-neutral (Apple, 1993).

A number of specifically educational ideas and assumptions have supported the broader view that schools, as institutions integral to our social structure, are guided by principles of fairness that are politically and socially blind. Nowhere is this more apparent than in efforts to provide a system of teacher preparation.

MAINSTREAM APPROACHES TO TEACHER PREPARATION

Though initially a male profession in the United States, teaching quickly became perceived as "women's work." This was due to a number of interlocking factors: (1) men increasingly were provided access to higher-status professions, with a resultant fear of teacher shortages; (2) women could be hired for a fraction of the cost of men, and were considered more easily controllable by male supervisors and administrators; (3) women's "natural" proclivities toward nurturance and a kind of moral guidance provided ideological support for a gender-specific view of teaching; (4) women were largely excluded from the high-status professions, and denied admission to the elite institutions of higher education that provided access to such professions; (5) the social construction of woman as more emotional/less inclined toward reason, nurturant toward children but not inclined to participate in political discourse and action, made her a "natural" educator, especially of young children; and (6) a patriarchal structure within schools supported the social dynamics of inequality and power in American society generally (Beyer, Feinberg, Pagano, & Whitson, 1989; Hoffman, 1981; Mattingly, 1975; Warren, 1989). Making teaching a "woman's profession" was a complex process, involving social and cultural values and ideologies as well as perceived educational needs. The early public school teacher was often valued for her ability to provide the necessary moral guidance for unruly, poor, and immigrant children, whose home life was seen as the source of many problems for them and the society at large. The woman teacher's guiding hand was felt to be necessary both for the good of the child and for the stability of the social order (Nasaw, 1979).

Since the opportunity of pursuing a teaching career in the early development of our public school system was characteristically seized by people excluded from the elite higher education establishment, early teachers tended to come from the working classes. This provided a sense of connection with their students, who typically came from similar backgrounds. In addition to issues of gender, then, the makeup of the early teaching force reflected the social class distinctions that were realities of American economic life. Just as normal school training might provide an avenue for professional mobility for women—even if partially compromised by the patriarchal structure of schools and sexism in society—their work with students might begin the path to opportunity for their charges. Thus, the teaching profession offered genuine opportunities for women who sought something other than marriage or factory work—as circumscribed as those opportunities, from some vantage points, were. As Nancy Hoffman (1981) puts it, in the 19th century teaching "moved into a position that it would hold for the rest of the century, and on into modern times: less than equal in status to male professions, *and* a source of satisfaction and power for women" (pp. 15–16, emphasis in original).

While de jure segregation was officially declared unconstitutional with the *Brown* decision of 1954, de facto segregation persists. This has implications for both the composition of the teaching profession and the everyday practices of schools (the content of the curriculum, patterns of student interaction and language usage, and measures of academic performance). In the 19th century, African-American slaves struggled to become literate in spite of laws that forbade such activities. After the end of the Civil War, wealthy white landowners rebelled against the idea of a state-supported system of education for African-Americans, believing it would upset the "natural evolution of society" (Anderson, 1988). Today, as over a century ago, many urban, mostly African-American public schools remain underfunded and understaffed, with all the consequences this has for those children and the society generally (Kozol, 1991). And while the need for more minority teachers is great, especially given the problems of urban, largely segregated schools, comparatively few students of color choose teaching as a career (Gordon, 1994). The legacy of our past lives on in these contemporary realities.

An emphasis on students' moral uplift—largely to be acquired via the example provided through the character of the teacher and not through direct instruction—was central to the developing picture of the teacher in the second quarter of the 19th century. Yet this was a politically and pedagogically conservative moral training that sought to exclude contentious ideas and people from the classroom. Public schools were to teach the common virtues in a way that would guarantee social harmony and self-reliance within a changing social and economic order. Fearing the disruptions of social change that were taking place in Europe and elsewhere, Horace Mann, for example, advocated the creation of a common American character through schooling that would defuse political and intellectual conflict. As he said in his 12th and final report to the Massachusetts Board of Education in 1848, "If the tempest of political strife were to be let loose upon our Common Schools, they would be overwhelmed with sudden ruin. . . . A preliminary advantage, indispensable to ultimate success, will be the appointment of a teacher of the true faith" (Cremin, 1957, pp. 94–95). As a moral guide, the working-class, white, often religiously trained woman was to provide a model of virtue to which students might aspire. Proper school activities themselves were believed to be non-partisan and non-political, both in terms of their status within the classroom and their consequences for children. Helping prospective teachers adjust to such a system of schooling became a primary obligation of teacher educators.

The preparation of teachers has frequently focused on providing a kind of technical competence aimed at helping students "fit in" to the current realities of schooling.[1] From the normal school movement of the 19th century to the more contemporary concern for providing "survival skills" (Fuller, 1969) to future teachers, to the call for the deinstitutionalization of teacher education in favor of a school-based apprenticeship system, programs that have fostered theoretical insight and inquiry have frequently been dismissed as lacking in useful knowledge or as too destabilizing. For teaching has been seen by many as a profession requiring the sort of competence that is only possible to develop within the immediate context of schooling itself, since this is where teachers must "prove" themselves. Within this orientation, teacher education is concerned with helping prospective teachers acquire appropriate techniques and strategies, manage and monitor classroom interactions, ensure academic achievement (largely through test scores of one sort or another), and create activities that are socially desirable and developmentally appropriate. Such a view of professional development can best be accomplished by putting into effect a skilled apprenticeship system within which "neophytes" gradually come to acquire the skills and dispositions of "Master Teachers."[2] This view of teaching has recently led to proposals, notably in the United Kingdom, to make the preparation of teachers largely the responsibility of the schools themselves, and not departments and schools of education in the university (Poppleton & Pullin, 1992).

The long-standing dualism between ideas and actions that has typified Western culture, with "higher education" and schools occupying different domains, makes universities appear as lofty citadels of theoretical discourse poorly suited to the preparation of schoolteachers, who need a kind of vocational/technical training. Given the deep-seated antagonism between theory and practice, in schools and elsewhere, and the class-, gender-, and race-influenced history of teaching and of teacher education sketched above, schools and programs to prepare teachers have tended to foster a kind of instrumentalism, wedded to various social conventions and ideological constructs.

An acceleration in the deskilling of teaching observed and analyzed over the last few decades is in keeping with many of the assumptions that guided the first normal and common schools, and is fully understandable only within the dynamics of power that characterize U.S. society (Beyer & Apple, 1988; Tabakin & Densmore, 1986). As more and more decisions are taken out of teachers' hands, with classroom activities bounded by norms of accountability for standardized test scores and classroom order, and the use of behavioristic, technical languages and values dominates (Huebner, 1975), teaching becomes increasingly routinized, the creative, visionary voices of teachers muted. For example, when behavior modification techniques are utilized to maximize students' "time on task"; when commercial curriculum materials dominate, reducing the teacher to a technician who simply follows the step-by-step directions provided by elaborate instructional manuals; when the school day is fragmented into discrete time blocks that isolate subject matters and undermine student projects; when the demands on teachers' time cut short opportunities for reflection and inquiry; and when the uninterpreted results of standardized test scores are used to make summary judgments about teachers' effectiveness, the classroom becomes a place of monotony, even drudgery. This pattern of deskilling has of course been furthered by the increased use of textbooks and mechanistic approaches to curriculum making (Apple, 1987; Franklin, 1986; Kliebard, 1992). The effects of deskilling on the day-to-day realities of teaching are nicely captured by Ushma Shah in Chapter 3, in the section entitled, "Deskilled: The Teacher as Puppet"; and, in Chapter 5, by Noelle Hawk Jaddaoui, as she discusses the use of basal readers in the section called, "Pressures Affecting My Classroom Practice."

The routinization of teaching has been furthered by approaches to teacher education that are themselves deskilled in important ways. In fact there is more than a little similarity between the normal school training of the last century and the practices of many contemporary teacher education programs—including some proposals for their reform. Teacher education programs have become more field-based, partly through the mandates of state departments of education. Student teaching has become an apparently universal component of teacher preparation. And since some kind of classroom proficiency is a requirement for teachers, this is both understandable and appropriate. Increasingly, however, educational regulatory bodies are mandating extensive experience in schools as a prerequisite to student teaching. As a result of such mandates, teacher educators have created practica, classroom observation modules, and field-based courses or course components, and have encouraged student-mentor relationships involving public school teachers. The rationale for these activities is often well intentioned. Yet it seems likely that one outcome is the unreflective socialization of prospective teachers into the accepted norms, mores, and folkways of the profession as it is currently practiced.

This socialization process is frequently undertaken in the name of lessening students' anxieties and fears, and developing a sense of "professionalism" among future teachers. Though such a rationale seems commonsensical, there are consequences to the socialization of prospective teachers that are problematic, just as there are assumptions in it that must be critically examined. Teacher education students, quite understandably, want to succeed in the environment in which they plan to spend their professional career and, just as understandably, they want to be *seen* as succeeding. One result is that students may tend either to adopt, or "strategically comply" with, the norms and values they observe in classrooms that are required for institutionally defined success (Lacey, 1977).

To the extent that preservice students see schools as "the reality" awaiting them, to be accommodated and adapted to rather than utilized as a forum for inquiry, investigation, and critique, they may well come to see college courses that emphasize reflection and critical engagement as irrelevant—a charge frequently levied against courses in the social foundations of education (Beyer & Zeichner, 1982). When this attitude is widely shared, professional preparation programs become perceived as a largely irrelevant academic journey on the road to the real, practical job of teaching in the schools. The nature of teacher education programs that highlight technical competence and professional socialization is furthered as well by the gendered nature of teaching and the patterns of deskilling with which it is associated, as already discussed. When teacher preparation is guided by a utilitarian, technical/vocational, assimilation approach, the educational status quo and the social realities with which they are aligned are furthered.

The rejection of a substantive theoretical background for prospective teachers, and the substitution of an apprenticeship-oriented program, raises a central question about the politics of teacher preparation and the aims by which it should be guided (Beyer, 1993). One of the important dimensions of critical educational inquiry is that it raises questions about the justifiability of current practices—whether from a historical, philosophical, sociological, psychological, or moral point of view—and the ends they serve. Such inquiry fosters both reflection on current educational activities and a basis for alternative directions, while rejecting an unexamined embrace of the status quo.

CRITICAL INQUIRY AND THE PREPARATION OF TEACHERS

The values, social patterns, and educational policies that have moved us in an educationally and socially conservative direction fostering deskilled teaching, the silencing of teachers, and the vocationalization of teacher preparation have always been challenged, of course—indeed, from their earliest appearance. So have the assertions that schools are meritocratic institutions designed to foster individual betterment and social progress in ways that are apolitical and non-ideological, and that women are naturally inclined toward nurturance and moral guidance. These challenges have taken many forms, including theoretical analyses by academics, the efforts of teacher educators, the work of teachers and administrators in the public schools, and the actions of parents and community members. The very naturalness of schooling, including its pretension to political and ideological neutrality, has been challenged by contemporary educational inquiry— especially as related to curriculum, pedagogy, and teacher education. Critical inquiry in education has sought to contextualize educational policies and school practices so that we may understand the ends of education and their sometimes overlooked relations with the dynamics of American society.

One fundamental perspective within this literature, which forms a significant basis for inquiry-oriented programs of teacher education, is that the means and ends of education are neither created *sui generis* nor constructed according to scientific principles that embody transcendent truths. Inquiry-oriented teacher education of a critical variety recognizes that school policies and practices are intimately and unavoidably tied to some conception of what is regarded as socially good or necessary, to political actions and appropriate forms of civic life, to cultural forms as means of symbolic expression that affect our individual and collective identity, and to some notion of productive work, which is often thought to constitute the central purpose of public education. To suppose that choices regarding teaching practices are based exclusively on considerations attached to individuated psyches is to misunderstand the fundamentally social character of education.[3] Disputes like those that swirled around New York City's multicultural curriculum, "Children of the Rainbow," culminating in the firing of Chancellor Joseph Fernandez (Kantrowitz, 1992), are protracted and heated precisely because they involve at least two kinds of frequently contentious political and ethical disputes: who should control what our children read, see, and value, and what vision of the good life our schools should promulgate. To challenge conventional answers to these questions is, as Chancellor Fernandez found out, risky business.

There are serious and sometimes devastating consequences that follow from maintaining the educational status quo. For instance, consider the way knowledge is transmitted through the school curriculum. A number of scholars have shown how a "selective tradition" (Apple, 1990; Apple & Weis, 1983; Williams, 1961) operates to shape both the content and form of curriculum materials—denying access to certain ideas and perspectives while validating others. Of course choices must always be made in constructing a curriculum. Yet the selectivity that gives shape to the school curriculum is neither politically disinterested nor socially benign. In helping maintain existing social relations, a selective tradition serves to support the interests of powerful groups while denying the authenticity and value of "minority" viewpoints and groups. Again, social values, forms of personal demeanor, and interaction patterns are reinforced through a dominant hidden curriculum, providing for students both a sense of "the way things are" in classrooms and an introduction to social expectations that will help shape their futures (Apple, 1975; Henry, 1965; Jackson, 1968; Nasaw, 1979; Vallance, 1977). The relative stability of many teaching practices over time and across geographic regions—increasingly reflecting the deskilling of teachers' labor—attests to the social usefulness of those practices and their consequences (Cuban, 1984; Sirotnik, 1988). In short, there is ample evidence that educational institutions have been instrumental in maintaining patterns of social, economic, and cultural power through the dominance of belief structures and the distribution of skills, information, and "legitimate"/useful knowledge (Apple, 1982a; Feinberg, 1983). As a cultural institution and a part of the material and ideological apparatuses that make up the contemporary state, schools have been shaped by, and in turn have helped give shape to, economic, political, and social realities that have helped maintain patterns of exploitation and oppression. It is no wonder that Henry Giroux (1992) begins a recent book by telling the reader that, while his previous work focused on educational institutions and their possible contributions to critical citizenship,

> I no longer believe that the struggle over education can be reduced to these sites, nor do I believe that pedagogy as a form of political, moral, and social production can be addressed primarily as a matter of schooling. . . . I vastly underestimated [in previous writing] both the structural and ideological constraints under which teachers labor as well as the hold that the prevailing conservatism has in shaping the curriculum and vision of most schools of education in the United States. (p. 1)

The pitfalls of identifying education and pedagogy exclusively with schooling have often been noted. It is also true that we must avoid being naive when suggesting that schools need not reproduce society in forms that serve the interests of the most powerful segments of U.S. society. Yet the undifferentiated pessimism expressed by Giroux (1992) seems, based on my experiences, premature and unfounded.

The literature on the role of schooling as a force for economic and cultural reproduction has been immensely helpful in clarifying the role of schooling in American social life. Still, empirical, qualitative, and narrative accounts of school practice, and normatively guided alternative conceptions of teaching and curriculum, have attenuated some of the earlier work in social reproduction theory that saw schools in functional terms (Bowles & Gintis, 1976). While there are structural constraints on educational institutions and policies that serve the purposes of reproducing economic and cultural realities, the ability of students, teachers, and administrators to actively resist or rechannel those constraints has been highlighted in a good deal of recent literature (Apple, 1982a; Everhart, 1983; Giroux, 1983; Ross, Cornett, & McCutcheon, 1992; Weiler & Mitchell, 1992; Willis, 1980). We have also become more sophisticated in understanding the contradictory forces at work in the state and culture generally, and more aware of the extent to which hegemonic beliefs and patterns of action do not automatically appear and oppress their victims, but instead emerge out of processes of struggle whose outcome cannot be predicted. These realizations have led to a revision in some earlier critical perspectives about the role of schooling in American social life. Such reappraisals parallel other movements to incorporate traditions of educational scholarship that deal with race, gender, ethnicity, and sexual orientation, as well as social class (Apple, 1982b; Dale, Esland, & Macdonald, 1980; McCarthy, 1990; Sears, 1992; Williams, 1977).

Inquiry-oriented teacher education moves beyond critique of existing educational and social realities, to creating educational practices aimed at social justice rather than stability, participation rather than silencing and exclusion, liberation rather than domination, equity rather than exploitation. Teaching is seen as a moral calling that necessitates alternative forms of pedagogy and curriculum, novel approaches to evaluation, and reconceived forms of teacher preparation. Such understandings are possible only if we contextualize educational activities, and if we see the province of teacher education and the domain of schooling as related to new social possibilities.

THEORY AND PRACTICE IN TEACHER EDUCATION: TAKING IT PERSONALLY

I encountered many of the ideas and issues discussed in the preceding section during my graduate school work at the University of Wisconsin–Madison and, for a shorter period, at the University of Illinois at Urbana-Champaign. It was only after receiving my doctorate in 1981 that I began to reflect more comprehensively and practically on the concrete programmatic and pedagogical implications of the perspectives I continued to develop. I accepted a position at Knox College as coordinator of elementary education in the fall of that year. Since then I have attempted to sponsor courses and programs that would create new approaches to teacher education that would be sensitive to the issues and ideas already discussed.[4] Along the way, numerous alterations in my thinking took place, as I worked to devise approaches to teaching and schooling that would help prepare students to engage in analyses, forms of inquiry, and projects that would further the struggle for social justice, the common good, and moral and political values such as those associated with participatory democracy. I have learned a great deal from the students I have been fortunate enough to work with, as exemplified by the authors of the central chapters of this book.

It is worth noting that Knox College was founded in 1837 by a religiously affiliated group that sought, among other things, to combine mental and manual labor, and to work for the abolition of slavery. The mission of the college has been, and continues to be, based on several interlocking principles. First, the commitment of the college to social justice, especially with respect to issues of social class, race/ethnicity, and gender, lies close to the core of the reasons for the college's founding (Muelder, 1984). Second, the provision of a quality liberal education is a defining element of the college. For students this involves asking important, fundamental questions about perennial and more contemporary issues; for faculty, the opportunity to engage in research that furthers the liberal arts mission of the college as it enhances teaching. Third, the emphasis on helping students communicate effectively with each other, to think carefully and critically about their own life situations, to connect intellectual engagement with moral responsibility, and to take increased responsibility for their education is a distinguishing feature of the college.

One result of this emphasis is that students generally decide to attend Knox not to gain access to career paths but to acquire habits of heart and mind that are fostered by a liberal education. From the first-year seminar required of all students, they are engaged in classroom discussions about a host of intellectual, moral, and political issues. In addition, there is ample opportunity for students to organize activities and sponsor events on campus dealing with contemporary issues. As a result, even students who enroll at Knox with the intent of being certified to teach in the public schools are perhaps more open to debate about educational ideas, less narrowly fixed on obtaining a credential.

The teacher education program in existence at Knox on my arrival in the early 1980s was fairly conventional. It combined a class on contemporary educational issues with courses in educational psychology and in the methodology of the various content areas of elementary or secondary education, ending with a requirement for student teaching. Field experiences were also included in the program, which apparently fostered professional socialization and a tacit acceptance of current classroom realities and professional norms. The role of teacher education—a presumably vocational/technical domain, after all—within a liberal arts context is always problematic. This was the case at Knox when I started teaching there in the fall of 1981.

I began thinking about the possibilities of articulating a conceptual foundation for the study of education during those early years. Such a foundation might do two things: first, acknowledge the value of educational studies as itself a liberal field of inquiry, one that is relevant for students whether or not they choose to pursue teaching as a profession; and second, provide a basis for teacher preparation that would diverge from the historical and contemporary mainstream, as outlined above. It might then be possible to integrate educational studies with other areas of the college, while providing an underpinning for teacher preparation that would ground it in social, political, and moral questions that are fundamental to the operation of classrooms.[5] Broadly speaking, I began to develop a perspective on the nature of education as a field of study that is:

1. Constituted by methodological pluralism and an interdisciplinary openness that allows students of education to combine insights and forms of analysis from a number of domains, including history, philosophy, sociology, literature, and psychology
2. Dedicated to considering the ways in which knowledge, values, and forms of consciousness are transmitted so as to promote social continuity, and to considering a critical perspective on these processes that might lead to social change
3. Concerned in a vital way with the practices of schooling, though schools are not the only institutions involved in education, and though educational scholarship should not narrowly restrict itself to current forms of school practice
4. Instrumental in developing a contextualized awareness (historically as well as socially) of current patterns in U.S. society and their relationship to educational issues and practices
5. Committed to linking analysis and reflection with proposals for redirection and action

The approach to the teacher education program that emerged over the ensuing years sought to raise as central themes the dynamics of social inequality (especially by gender, social class, ethnicity, race, and age) and their implications for schooling and teaching. As central dynamics related to the function of schools in maintaining (or altering) patterns of social continuity, these forms of inequality are directly implicated in school processes such as tracking or ability grouping, the design and dissemination of curricula, patterns of pupil socialization, and student evaluation. An awareness of such social dynamics was accompanied by the development of a critical perspective that was incorporated into virtually all coursework and practical experiences in schools. Instead of classroom observations and activities serving as sites for socialization into a profession whose parameters could be taken for granted, they became avenues for critical analysis, reflection, and action. The nature of appropriate "field experiences" changed as well, both in focus and format. The program came to include work in social service agencies, homeless shelters, centers devoted to supporting victims of domestic violence, literacy programs, and so forth (Beyer, 1991). As Ushma Shah discusses in Chapter 3, her tutoring experiences in a literacy program provided a concrete example of how reflection on social issues and current realities can be combined with practical action in and on the world.

More generally, in addition to analysis and critique, our programs as a whole emphasized the essentially moral responsibility of teachers to create, implement, and evaluate alternative curricula and pedagogy. Building on the burgeoning literature on teacher empowerment and the reflective practitioner (Grimmett & Erickson, 1988; Schön, 1983, 1987; Smyth, 1989; Zeichner & Liston, 1987), I sought to provide opportunities for morally, politically, and socially informed choices by students. Helping them develop a personal and social "platform" (Barone, 1988) became a central purpose of teacher education. Such a platform contains social and educational principles in which a student not only believes but on which he or she is prepared to act. It provides something on which to stand, as it were, as the realities of classrooms are examined and responded to.

The reformed teacher education curriculum that was gradually implemented was centered on helping students develop an informed personal and social praxis (Freire, 1973)—an integration of theoretical insight and practical action that combined daily life in classrooms with more global social, moral, and political concerns. This would reorient our coursework and also alter the nature of field experiences in the schools and, it was hoped, students' teaching experiences once they were employed. Our courses continually emphasized:

1. The need for students to avoid uncritically accepting the ideas, claims, and interests of others, and instead to actively "claim" their own education (Rich, 1979), and to engage in research projects of various kinds

2. The importance of developing philosophical approaches to teaching and curriculum in accord with which more concrete pedagogical and curricular activities could be undertaken in schools
3. A view of schools and teaching as embedded within historical and social parameters that often had been largely obscured through a reliance on behaviorist psychology and objectivist epistemologies that are seriously flawed (Beyer, 1988)
4. A realization that the current world of schooling is only one among several possibilities, which often serves the interests of certain groups at the expense of others
5. The importance of a synthetic or synoptic vision that is critical of current realities in schools without becoming dismissive, and productive of alternative approaches without being naively idealistic

Our efforts reflected the value and trust we placed in students to become autonomous, morally engaged, politically sensitive, reflective teachers who could take and argue for positions and actions that were well formulated, while remaining open and responsive to those whose ideas diverged from their own.

The orientation to teacher education that emerged through this process of reflection and reform can be summarized by noting that I came to regard teaching as "a field of reflective moral action," which provides a unifying theme. There are specific as well as more global aspects of this orientation that can be outlined.

Teaching as Moral/Political Action

In some ways a focus on the moral qualities of teacher deliberation can be stated in negative terms. It grows out of my sense as a teacher and teacher educator that, as teaching becomes more and more deskilled and routinized, attention to the valuative dimensions of education is often lacking. Within such a climate, the ways in which teaching is importantly constituted by value judgments become obscured, replaced by technical measures and standards that provide a veneer of objectivity and neutrality that hides the political and value-laden nature of school practice.

In a more positive sense, a primary moral obligation of teachers is to see the ends of education as neither settled nor extraneous to their professional life, and to see the complexities and responsibilities embedded in the ongoing, day-to-day project of rethinking the purposes of schooling. To the extent that we regard the ends of education and schooling as unproblematic or irrelevant, we limit our students to an instrumentalism that cuts short opportunities for moral engagement. If we are to avoid such instrumentalism, teacher educators must provide opportunities for reflection on current school practice and the ends it serves, as well as support for articulating alternative practices that respect students' integrity as moral beings and their abilities as social actors. This was a central component of the approach to teacher education I helped construct.

The current literature is replete with an awareness of racial, gender, and social class inequities, as well as multicultural perspectives that seek to address those inequities in classrooms (American Association of University Women, 1992; Anderson, 1988; Heath, 1983; hooks, 1989; Lomotey, 1990; Ogbu, 1987; Sleeter, 1991). Yet we cannot hope to really educate public school pupils who now live on the margins of schooling and society if we do not address the reasons for continued inequalities and the lack of connection between students' present and future lives, and if we do not clarify the meaning of genuinely democratic communities and how they can be developed. It was a dedication to educating such pupils that led many of my students to work with English as a Second Language and bilingual education populations in the schools. Erin Roche, Krista Sorensen, and Noelle Hawk Jaddaoui, three of the chapter authors of this book, were drawn to working with those students. In addition, many students chose to complete their student teaching experience in the inner-city schools of Chicago. This was facilitated by the Urban Education Program, under the auspices of the consortium of liberal arts schools of which Knox is a part. They chose to work with marginalized students as a way of making a difference in their lives, and as a way of working toward social justice. All of the authors included in this volume have chosen to work with such students, in one way or another, in one context or another, as a concrete expression of their commitment to moral and democratic practice and to the welfare of children. As Mary Cunat puts it in Chapter 8, it is the "have nots" of the social and educational system "that especially need access to and experience with democratic education."

Especially for poor students and students of color, teaching as a field of moral action requires a theory of social power that is grounded in critical educational inquiry, and in an understanding of the possibilities for democratic participation in reconstructing social reality. Such a theory can help teachers understand the dynamics of student interaction, curriculum development and pedagogy, evaluation, professionalism, and so on, as these arise in classrooms. A theoretical perspective of this sort is vital if we—teachers, teacher educators, and students—are to collaboratively undertake actions that will lead to the development of genuinely democratic and egalitarian classrooms and social orders.

TEACHING AND THE POLITICS OF HOPE

This book is founded on the idea that schools can be, and often are, a progressive force in American society. It serves as a testimony to the value of hope that is not naive, and to possibility that is always "becoming." Indeed this has been something of a plank in American educational thought from the very beginning of our country—even though what has counted as social progress has frequently been skewed through the ability of powerful groups to protect their own interests by redefining a progressive educational agenda. From social reconstructionists in the second quarter of this century like George S. Counts (1932) and Harold Rugg (1939), and to some extent, before that time, John Dewey (1916), to more contemporary advocates of the progressive possibilities for schooling (Apple, 1982a; Bastian, Fruchter, Gittell, Greer, & Haskins, 1986; Beyer & Liston, 1996; Freire, 1973; Giroux, 1983; Greene, 1978; Liston, 1988; Stanley, 1992; Wood, 1992) there has existed the claim and hope that schooling could be a force for social betterment.

The belief that significant educational and social change is possible has been fueled by a number of forces—both theoretical and practical. A key impetus has come through writings that have critiqued our commonsense notions of democracy—a subject that is central to this volume and that the authors further. A number of writers have critically investigated the meanings of democracy that infuse political discourse and social and educational practices, and have suggested alternative conceptions of what democratic life might entail. Benjamin Barber (1984, 1992), for example, has drawn a useful distinction between protectionist/weak democracy and participatory/strong democracy that challenges many of our current assumptions about the meaning of democracy within our social formation. Instead of turning over decision-making power to a supposed elite that will protect our interests, Barber argues for more broad-based participation by all of us on matters affecting the social good, and the provision of a material base for all that is a prerequisite to such participation. Similarly, Carole Pateman (1970) has analyzed possible levels of political participation—pseudo, partial, and full—and the social conditions necessary for the enactment of the kind of full participation that is consistent with a revised notion of democracy. Amy Gutmann (1987) has proposed a democratic framework for the reconstruction of educational institutions and their governance that emphasizes at the public school level non-repression and non-discrimination, while helping create the necessary democratic character in students. Jane J. Mansbridge (1980) has disclosed how the town meeting of New England, and other more participatory commitments to decision making, offer a conception of democratic values that differ in crucial ways from the emphases on electoral politics, campaign rhetoric, and exhortations to vote in national and local elections that unfortunately tend to be equated with democratic forms of life. This body of literature has posited alternative visions of democracy that call into question the meanings we typically ascribe to it. Freire's (1973) emphasis on "integration" with the world, rather than "adapting" to it, is relevant to this alternative understanding of democracy. As Freire puts it, "integration results from the capacity to adapt oneself to reality *plus* the critical capacity to make choices and to transform that reality" (p. 4, emphasis in original). To become an integrated person is not only to understand the worlds in which we live and work, but to become the kind of person who will take part in shaping and reshaping those worlds. This emphasis on critique of current realities, and on participating in the re-creation of our worlds, is a central part of democratic life.

If we understand democracy in its strong or participatory sense, and wish to broaden the scope of participation beyond that which exists in many contemporary institutions, several claims can be made that have rather immediate consequences for education. If people are to have significant input into choices affecting their lives, they must develop the following:

1. The ability to analyze, critique, and evaluate options so that both short- and long-term consequences can be considered
2. A forum for the public discussion of issues and ideas, since it is through such discussion that we create, clarify, and reevaluate our own positions and understand the perspectives of others
3. The opportunity and ability to locate relevant information, and to uncover multiple interpretations of it that provide new meanings
4. The habit of coming together as equals, living in genuine communities, to make public decisions, within which we are not coerced or manipulated by "experts" with access to forms of allegedly private and specialized knowledge
5. A moral commitment to the common good, and community, that transcends both individual self-interest and emotivism and exposes the tendency for more powerful individuals and groups to manipulate and cajole the rest of us (Bellah, Madsen, Sullivan, Swidler, & Tipton, 1985, 1991; Carnoy, Shearer, & Rumberger, 1983; Cohen & Rogers, 1983; Raskin, 1986; Selznick, 1992)

Teaching for Democratic Values

These ideas have important implications for educational practice. While much has been written about the importance of fostering students' "critical thinking," what this actually means is often quite vague, amounting to a method of problem solving that deviates comparatively little from current school practice. Given what has already been said about a revitalized sense of democracy, we might encourage a kind of critical thinking that will help students develop their ability to get beyond the "surface realities" (Greene, 1978) of situations. This is the kind of critical reflection on the "taken-for-granted" or routine of everyday school life that Mary Cunat engaged in with her fifth graders. As she outlines in Chapter 8, she actively encouraged her students to think through, with her, the "common sense" of everyday school practice, challenging and altering it when possible in ways that fostered students' own "integration" with the school world (Freire, 1973).

Another example of critical inquiry on day-to-day life that has relevance for an altered conception of democracy involves teachers' highlighting the critical problems many students face everyday—real and threatened violence, physical and sexual abuse, racism, or the loss of a loved one, for example. This is just the sort of active involvement with students that Joni Garlock achieved with "Jill," a student who had been sexually abused. In Chapter 4, Joni outlines how Jill, unable to deal with her ordeal, confided in her about that abusive relationship. Together, they went through the process of notifying the authorities and working through that trauma, thus extending a sense of caring beyond the confines of the school. Such actions illustrate the importance of teachers as more than academic specialists, and demonstrate how they can help students deal with the painful realities that are often crucial parts of their lives.

If we are to help students develop democratic characters, we must encourage the discussion of moral issues, and provide the kind of information and perspectives, as well as non-sanctioned interpretations of events, that are normally excluded from the curriculum (see, for instance, Chicago Religious Task Force on Central America, 1991; Rethinking Schools, 1991). Teaching in a fifth-grade classroom that was ethnically and economically diverse, Ushma Shah helped students critically investigate portions of the school curriculum. As she describes in Chapter 3, she was required to teach a unit on Islam based on a textbook that highlighted a militaristic image that denied both cultural diversity and the current lives of Muslims. Ushma used the required chapter as a launching point for students to begin to critique their own texts. This led to a more wide-ranging discussion of bias in school materials, why it exists, and what can be done in response to it. This segment provides an insightful discussion of how a "selective tradition" actually worked its way through the fifth grade in which Ushma was teaching.

As critical teachers committed to a participatory form of democratic action, we might foster the values of cooperation, moral reasoning toward a common good, and a forum for the expression of opposing views that would help create such a revitalized democracy. In Chapter 2, Erin Roche discusses his attempts to develop a sense of community. There he raises a complex, difficult problem of the power dynamics that are present in virtually all classrooms. In a setting where differences are not always valued and individually defined standards for success tend to dominate, Erin's efforts to create a cooperative environment are crucial reminders of the importance of sharing power with students. Such efforts to create settings in which students encourage and respect each other are crucial for the establishment of participatory communities.

As previously noted, many authors have exposed the actual contradictions, resistances, and alternative directions that take place in many classrooms (Everhart, 1983; Willis, 1980). These studies have documented already existing actions that could foster school change and help us see the actual complexities of classrooms more clearly. They provide suggestive ways to develop alternative theoretical frameworks and divergent school practices. But this requires a flexibility on the part of teachers that is not always in evidence, as well as an openness to criticism. As Katie Poduska says in Chapter 7, reflecting on the fluid nature of genuine teaching, "growth does not come without change and change, at least in the classroom, is not evoked without challenge. . . . I have learned that easy teaching is not always the most productive teaching for either myself or my students." Just as a participatory, democratic world is socially constructed and thus not always predictable or easy, so too is the genuinely democratic classroom, as Katie makes clear.

A number of school reform measures have been implemented that aim at providing autonomy for teachers and the empowerment of both the inhabitants of schools and the communities of which they are a part. The Chicago school reforms, for example, gave teachers and Local School Councils the opportunity to make decisions about curricula, budgets, and school leaders that held the promise of altering long-standing patterns of control in schools (Ayers, 1990; Hess, 1991; McKersie, 1993; Mirel, 1993). Such reform measures may help alter the trend toward the deskilling of teaching, and assist in the movement toward schooling as a vehicle for social justice. Krista Sorensen provides compelling evidence of teacher empowerment and its concrete meanings for practice in Chapter 6. In order to work toward empowerment, Krista says, a teacher must first have a vision that is open to reexamination—a central purpose of critically oriented teacher education, as discussed above. in addition, both Krista and her students have been "risk takers"—another vital element of a genuinely participatory, democratic classroom, as she outlines.

The sense of isolation for many teachers who embody non-mainstream sentiments can be quite taxing—a likely occurrence about which I worried a great deal as I worked to create and implement a critically oriented teacher education program. The lack of support, even hostility, from others—teachers, administrators, parents, even students themselves, I know from my own experiences in the public schools—can be overwhelming. Combating this sense of loneliness and isolation is sometimes quite difficult, especially in the early years when teachers are trying to develop and find opportunities to express their own voice. Noelle Hawk Jaddaoui conveys her own attempt to build the sort of bridges that invigorate her teaching activities and that support the sort of risk taking that is essential for innovative teaching. In Chapter 5, she outlines the struggles that creative, committed teachers go through as they create their own identity and remain connected to others and to moral principles.

CONCLUSION

There remains an important gap among critical educational scholarship of the sort that was explored earlier, the commitments of progressive educational scholars, the informed hope of creating alternative educational and social possibilities, and descriptions of the actual practices that will give expression to concrete actions and value commitments. This book was undertaken to help fill that gap.

I first came to the idea for a volume such as this one out of the sense that there are numerous examples of committed, progressive, critically reflective work going on in schools that are not in wide circulation, despite the avowed importance of "voice" as this has been emphasized in the literature. I also knew, through ongoing contact with students and former students, that they were doing exciting, invigorating work in the classrooms in which they taught. Thus I began this venture in August 1992, with no real notion of how it might turn out. I corresponded with the authors included here (and with a number of other potential authors, who for varying reasons could not participate). I initially sent each of them a copy of the prospectus for this book, and asked for feedback on it and the project as a whole. I continued working on this project, long distance, during my sabbatical leave of 1992–1993. I received outlines and eventually drafts of chapters from the authors, and provided what I hoped would be valuable feedback on them. I circulated those drafts, as individual authors felt appropriate, to each of the other authors. Then in June 1993, we met in the living room of my home to discuss the book as a whole and each other's thinking and writing to date. Subsequently discussion meetings were held in Chicago, again to discuss individual chapters, share ideas and perspectives, support one another, and discuss future possibilities.

As work on the book progressed, we had the chance to share portions of it with others. In November 1993 a symposium was held as part of the annual meeting of the American Educational Studies Association. Entitled "Schooling for a Revitalized Democracy," it allowed four of the authors (Mary Cunat, Joni Garlock, Katie Poduska, and Erin Roche) to discuss the ideas that eventually resulted in chapters included here. Then in March 1994, a symposium was sponsored by the Professors of Curriculum, entitled "Curriculum for the 21st Century: Economic Productivity or Social Justice?" As a part of that symposium, Ushma Shah presented a number of ideas and perspectives taken from her teaching and from her chapter included here. As I write this, I am preparing to submit a symposium proposal to the American Educational Research Association, for their annual meeting in April 1996, that would feature several of the included authors.

At the end of Chapter 2, Erin Roche notes that "the youngest children—even eight- and nine-year-old, non-native English speakers—can . . . act as teachers, even to those who are called teachers. . . . The student and the teacher co-exist as both learners and teachers, not as isolated identities." Similarly, Noelle Hawk Jaddaoui discusses in Chapter 5 how her pupils engaged in Writing Workshop activities during which they became both teacher and student; and Krista Sorensen, describing the rain forest unit initiated by her students, acknowledges in Chapter 6 the things she learned from her fourth graders. These and similar examples provided by the authors in the pages that follow suggest not only the interdependency of teacher and student, but the fluidity of these roles, perhaps especially in a democratic, participatory, critical classroom.

Exactly so. I hope I have given my students as much as I have received from them. And I hope it is obvious that I am very proud of each of the contributors to this volume—as teachers and as people. They help give me strength to continue the sort of work discussed above—even on those days when patience and tolerance are in short supply, and progress seems elusive. They remain a source of hope and strength for me, just as I know they have been for their other students.

I invite you to join them in dialogue, struggle, and action.

NOTES

1. There were groups, though, even during the era in which teacher education institutions were being founded, arguing for a more scholarly approach to teacher preparation. See, for example, the discussion of the American Institute of Instruction in Mattingly (1975).

2. An important early essay on the inadequacy of an apprenticeship system for teacher education is Dewey, 1904.

3. This is not to deny that there are psychological elements to educational activities, and that individual experience plays a crucial role in educational encounters. As Dewey (1900/1956, 1902/1956) said some time ago, the fundamental problem of education is how to integrate the psychological and the social. My point here is that a view of teaching and schooling that does not contextualize activities and theories is inadequate.

4. These efforts took place primarily at Knox College, and to a lesser extent at Cornell College and the University of Rochester, and now at Indiana University. Though they were developed over many years, I avoid here complex details regarding chronology and professional affiliations. Since such matters would not add to the discussion in this section, I provide here a general outline of the programs and approaches I have tried to develop. I would like to acknowledge the important contributions of my former colleagues at Knox College: Bruce Strom, now the Director of the Graduate Program in Education at Carroll College, with whom I worked from 1981 through 1984; and Amy McAninch, now on the faculty at St. Mary College, with whom I worked in 1990–1991. In addition, Susan Laird, a current faculty member at the University of Oklahoma, was an invaluable colleague at Cornell College during 1987–1988 as we attempted to reconceptualize teacher education at that institution.

5. Many of these ideas are elaborated in Beyer et al., 1989.

REFERENCES

American Association of University Women. (1992). *How schools shortchange girls*. Washington, DC: American Association of University Women and the National Education Association.

Anderson, J. D. (1988). *The education of blacks in the south, 1860–1935*. Chapel Hill: University of North Carolina Press.

Apple, M. W. (1975). The hidden curriculum and the nature of conflict. In W. Pinar (Ed.), *Curriculum theorizing: The reconceptualists* (pp. 95–119). San Francisco: McCutchan.

Apple, M. W. (1982a). *Education and power*. Boston: Routledge & Kegan Paul.

Apple, M. W. (1982b). *Cultural and economic reproduction in education*. Boston: Routledge & Kegan Paul.

Apple, M. W. (1987). *Teachers and texts: A political economy of class and gender relations in education*. New York: Routledge and Kegan Paul.

Apple, M. W. (1990). *Ideology and curriculum* (2nd ed.). New York: Routledge.

Apple, M. W. (1993). *Official knowledge: Democratic education in a conservative age*. New York: Routledge.

Apple, M. W., & Weis, L. (1983). *Ideology and practice in schooling*. Philadelphia: Temple University Press.

Ayers, W. (1990, September 12). Today is a new beginning . . . for creative teachers. *Chicago Tribune*, Section I, p. 1.

Barber, B. (1984). *Strong democracy*. Berkeley: University of California Press.

Barber, B. (1992). *An aristocracy of everyone: The politics of education and the future of America*. New York: Ballantine Books.

Barone, T. E. (1988). Curriculum platforms and literature. In L. E. Beyer & M. W. Apple (Eds.), *The curriculum: Problems, politics, and possibilities* (pp. 140-165). Albany: State University of New York Press.

Bastian, A., Fruchter, N., Gittell, M., Greer, C., & Haskins, K. (1986). *Choosing equality: The case for democratic schooling*. Philadelphia: Temple University Press.

Bellah, R. N., Madsen, R., Sullivan, W. M., Swidler, A., & Tipton, S. M. (1985). *Habits of the heart: Individualism and commitment in American life*. Berkeley: University of California Press.

Bellah, R. N., Madsen, R., Sullivan, W. M., Swidler, A., & Tipton, S. M. (1991). *The good society*. New York: Alfred A. Knopf.

Bennett, W. (1994). *The de-valuing of America: The fight for our culture and our children*. New York: Touchstone Books.

Beyer, L. E. (1988). *Knowing and acting: Inquiry, ideology, and educational studies*. London: Falmer Press.

Beyer, L. E. (1991). Teacher education, reflective inquiry, and moral action. In B. R. Tabachnick & K. M. Zeichner (Eds.), *Issues and practices in inquiry-oriented teacher education* (pp. 113-129). London: Falmer Press.

Beyer, L. E. (1993). Teacher education and the politics of schooling. *Education Research and Perspectives, 20*(1), 1-12.

Beyer, L. E., & Apple, M. W. (1988). *The curriculum: Problems, politics, and possibilities*. Albany: State University of New York Press.

Beyer, L. E., Feinberg, W., Pagano, J. A., & Whitson, J. A. (1989). *Preparing teachers as professionals: The role of educational studies and other liberal disciplines*. New York: Teachers College Press.

Beyer, L. E., & Liston, D. P. (1996). *Curriculum in conflict: Social visions, educational agendas, and progressive school reform*. New York: Teachers College Press.

Beyer, L. E., & Zeichner, K. M. (1982). Teacher training and educational foundations: A plea for discontent. *Journal of Teacher Education, 33*(3), 18-23.

Bloom, A. (1987). *The closing of the American mind*. New York: Simon & Schuster.

Bowles, S., & Gintis, H. (1976). *Schooling in capitalist America*. New York: Basic Books.

Carnoy, M., Shearer, D., & Rumberger, R. (1983). *A new social contract*. New York: Harper and Row.

Chicago Religious Task Force on Central America. (1991). *Dangerous memories: Invasion and resistance since 1492*. Chicago: Chicago Religious Task Force on Central America.

Cohen, J., & Rogers, J. (1983). *On democracy*. New York: Penguin Books.

Counts, G. S. (1932). *Dare the schools build a new social order?* New York: Day.

Cremin, L. A. (1957). *The republic and the school: Horace Mann on the education of free men*. New York: Teachers College Press.

Cuban, L. (1984). *How teachers taught: Constancy and change in American classrooms 1890-1980*. New York: Longman.

Dale, R., Esland, G., & Macdonald, M. (1980). *Education and the state*. London: Routledge & Kegan Paul.

Dewey, J. (1900/1956). *The school and society*. Chicago: University of Chicago Press.

Dewey, J. (1902/1956). *The child and the curriculum*. Chicago: University of Chicago Press.

Dewey, J. (1904). The relation of theory to practice in education. In C. A. McMurry, (Ed.), *The third yearbook of the National Society for the Scientific Study of Education, part I, The relation of theory to practice in the education of teachers* (pp. 9–30). Chicago: University of Chicago Press.

Dewey, J. (1916). *Democracy and education: An introduction to the philosophy of education*. New York: Free Press.

Everhart, R. B. (1983). *Reading, writing and resistance*. Boston: Routledge & Kegan Paul.

Feinberg, W. (1983). *Understanding education: Toward a reconstruction of educational inquiry*. New York: Cambridge University Press.

Finn, C. (1991). *We must take charge: The schools and our future*. New York: Macmillan.

Franklin, B. (1986). *Building the American community: The school curriculum and the search for social control*. Bristol, PA: Falmer Press.

Freire, P. (1973). *Education for critical consciousness*. New York: Seabury Press.

Fuller, F. (1969). Concerns of teachers: A developmental conceptualization. *American Educational Research Journal, 6*(2), 207–226.

Giroux, H. A. (1983). *Theory and resistance in education*. South Hadley, MA: Bergin and Garvey.

Giroux, H. A. (1992). *Border crossings: Cultural workers and the politics of education*. New York: Routledge.

Gordon, J. A. (1994). Why students of color are not entering teaching: Reflections from minority teachers. *Journal of Teacher Education, 45*(5), 346–353.

Greene, M. (1978). *Landscapes of learning*. New York: Teachers College Press.

Grimmett, P., & Erickson, G. (1988). *Reflection in teacher education*. New York: Teachers College Press.

Gutmann, A. (1987). *Democratic education*. Princeton: Princeton University Press.

Heath, S. B. (1983). *Ways with words: Language, life, and work in communities and classrooms*. New York: Cambridge University Press.

Henry, J. (1965). *Culture against man*. New York: Vintage Books.

Hess, G. A., Jr. (1991). *School restructuring, Chicago style*. Newbury Park, CA: Corwin Press, Inc.

Hirsch, E. D. (1987). *Cultural literacy: What every American needs to know*. Boston: Houghton Mifflin.

Hoffman, N. (1981). *Woman's "true" profession: Voices from the history of teaching*. Old Westbury, NY: Feminist Press.

hooks, b. (1989). *Talking back*. Boston: South End Press.

Huebner, D. (1975). Curricular language and classroom meanings. In W. Pinar (Ed.), *Curriculum theorizing: The reconceptualists* (pp. 217–236). Berkeley: McCutchan.

Jackson, P. W. (1968). *Life in classrooms*. New York: Holt, Rinehart & Winston.

Kantrowitz, B. (1992, December 21). If he could make it here . . . *Newsweek*, p. 57.

Kliebard, H. M. (1992). *Forging the American curriculum: Essays in curriculum history and theory*. New York: Routledge.

Kozol, J. (1991). *Savage inequalities: Children in America's schools*. New York: Crown Publishers.

Lacey, C. (1977). *The socialization of teachers*. London: Methuen.

Liston, D. P. (1988). *Capitalist schools: Explanation and ethics in radical studies of schooling*. New York: Routledge.

Lomotey, K. (1990). *Going to school: The African-American experience*. Albany: State University of New York Press.

Lukes, S. (1973). *Individualism*. Oxford: Basil Blackwell.

McCarthy, C. (1990). *Race and curriculum: Social inequality and the theories and politics of difference in contemporary research on schooling*. New York: Falmer Press.

McKersie, W. S. (1993). Philanthropy's paradox: Chicago school reform. *Educational Evaluation and Policy Analysis, 15*(2), 109-128.

Mansbridge, J. J. (1980). *Beyond adversary democracy*. Chicago: University of Chicago Press.

Mattingly, P. (1975). *The classless profession: American schoolmen in the nineteenth century*. New York: New York University Press.

Mirel, J. (1993). School reform, Chicago style: Educational innovation in a changing urban context. *Urban Education, 28*(2), 116-149.

Muelder, Hermann, 1984. *Missionaries and muckrakers: The first hundred years of Knox College*. Urbana: University of Illinois Press.

Nasaw, D. (1979). *Schooled to order: A social history of public schooling in the United States*. New York: Oxford University Press.

Newman, F. (1970). *Clarifying public controversy: An approach to teaching social studies*. Boston: Little, Brown.

Ogbu, J. U. (1987). Variability in minority school performance: A problem in search of an explanation. *Anthropology and Education Quarterly, 18*, 312-334.

Pateman, C. (1970). *Participation and democratic theory*. New York: Cambridge University Press.

Poppleton, P., & Pullin, R. (1992). Distant voices: English teachers' views on change in initial teacher education. *Journal of Education for Teaching, 18*(2), 115-129.

Raskin, M. (1986). *The common good*. New York: Routledge and Kegan Paul.

Rethinking Schools (1991). *Rethinking Columbus: Teaching about the 500th anniversary of Columbus's arrival in America*. Milwaukee: Rethinking Schools.

Rich, A. (1979). *On lies, secrets, and silence: Selected prose, 1966-1978*. New York: W. W. Norton.

Ross, E. W., Cornett, J. W., & McCutcheon, G. (1992). *Teacher personal theorizing: Connecting curriculum practice, theory, and research*. Albany: State University of New York Press.

Rugg, H. (1939). *Democracy and the curriculum: The life and program of the American school.* New York: Appleton-Century Company.

Sarason, S. B. (1990). *The predictable failure of educational reform: Can we change the course before it's too late?* San Francisco: Jossey-Bass.

Schön, D. (1983). *The reflective practitioner.* New York: Basic Books.

Schön, D. (1987). *Educating the reflective practitioner.* San Francisco: Jossey-Bass.

Sears, J. T. (1992). *Sexuality and the curriculum: The politics and practices of sexuality education.* New York: Teachers College Press.

Selznick, P. (1992). *The moral commonwealth: Social theory and the promise of community.* Berkeley: University of California Press.

Shannon, P. (1988). *Broken promises: Reading instruction in 20th century America.* South Hadley, MA: Bergin and Garvey.

Sirotnik, K. A. (1988). What goes on in classrooms? Is this the way we want it? In L. E. Beyer & M. W. Apple (Eds.), *The curriculum: Problems, politics, and possibilities* (pp. 56–74). Albany: State University of New York Press.

Sleeter, C. E. (1991). *Empowerment through multicultural education.* Albany: State University of New York Press.

Smyth, J. (1989). Developing and sustaining critical reflection in teacher education. *Journal of Teacher Education, 40*(2), 2–9.

Stanley, W. B. (1992). *Curriculum for utopia: Social reconstructionism and critical pedagogy in the postmodern era.* Albany: State University of New York Press.

Tabakin, G., & Densmore, K. (1986). Teacher professionalization and gender analysis. *Teachers College Record, 88*(2), 257–279.

Vallance, E. (1977). Hiding the hidden curriculum: An interpretation of the language of justification in nineteenth-century educational reform. In A. A. Bellack & H. M. Kliebard (Eds.), *Curriculum and evaluation* (pp. 590–607). Berkeley: McCutchan.

Warren, D. (1989). *American teachers: Histories of a profession at work.* New York: Macmillan.

Weiler, K., & Mitchell, C. (1992). *What schools can do: Critical pedagogy and practice.* Albany: State University of New York Press.

Williams, R. (1961). *The long revolution.* London: Chatto and Windus.

Williams, R. (1977). *Marxism and literature.* Oxford: Oxford University Press.

Willis, P. (1980). *Learning to labour: How working class kids get working class jobs.* Westmead, Farnborough, Hampshire, England: Gower Publishing Company Limited.

Wood, G. H. (1992). *Schools that work: America's most innovative public education programs.* New York: Penguin Books.

Zeichner, K. M., & Liston, D. P. (1987). Teaching student teachers to reflect. *Harvard Educational Review, 57*(1), 23–48.

TWO

The Bumpy Bus Ride
to the Democratic Classroom

Erin Roche

As on every other morning of my summer English as a Second Language
Program, I sat at a student desk near the classroom door, greeting the third-
and fourth-grade English as a Second Language students as they came in. As
the children who arrived by bus filed in, I noticed that they were more excited and agitated than usual. They talked quickly to one another and play-
fully mimicked a bus driver and his passengers in tow. Their energetic anima-
tion, however, wasn't the only tip that something was different; the "bus
driver" unexpectedly turned sharply around a row of desks and several occu-
pants tumbled to the floor, though the "driver" continued unabated and un-
concerned. Sensing something behind the play, my cooperating teacher immediately began to make some inquiries of the students and soon uncovered the
fact that the students were actually the victims of reckless bus driving.

The students' ensuing stories frightened me; I was concerned for their
lives, of course, but also that they would experience this again without
knowing how to confront abusive power. After school that day, my cooperating teacher and I met for our daily discussion and lesson planning. I
suggested that we use a language experience activity to evaluate the incident and improve the situation. I thought we could establish the students'
version of what had happened and at the same time address the situation.
She agreed. So the following day I led the students in writing a letter to
the principal, explaining what had happened to the students and what they
wanted changed.

We gathered in a small circle on the rug in the back of the room; I sat
on a chair next to the large paper on which I would write the letter, and

the children huddled on the floor. I began by reminding them of their awful bus ride the day before.

"How many of you ride the bus?" I asked, and most of the hands in the room shot up.

"How many of you like to ride the bus?" The same hands reappeared.

"Who remembers the day you stopped suddenly and you fell from your bus seats?" Again, hands in the air.

"Who remembers the day the bus didn't come?" More hands.

"If you wrote to the principal, what would you say to him about these things?"

The students flooded me with answers: "Tell him that the bus is dangerous."

"The bus goes too fast around corners."

"There are strange people standing in the front of the bus."

And on and on. With more of my guiding questions, we had soon straightened the story out and began to write it down as a group: They provided the words, while I served as a grammatical and syntax filter. Three students volunteered to recopy the letter, and it was delivered that day.

Though the students obviously were led and encouraged by me, they were creating their own work and challenging authority. They cooperated in order to criticize a bus driver for his behavior and respectfully submitted the criticism to the principal in a letter. We had experienced democratic learning!

Because this event empowered students and was connected to genuine problem solving, it, together with other classroom possibilities, sparked thought about and helped give expression to my own democratic educational and social visions; they serve as examples for much of what I want to say in this chapter. What follows is an outline of the democratic beliefs and values I live by and a discussion of how classroom activities can further them. I also analyze some substantial barriers that impede the realization of these ideals, and offer the voice of relatively inexperienced teachers as reminders of patience and persistence in building these ideals.

SOCIAL AND EDUCATIONAL VISIONS
FOR AN EMPOWERED CITIZENRY

When writing my first history of education paper in college, I remember discovering the importance of the relationship between the classroom and a democratic society (Roche, 1991). The paper was about antebellum women frontier teachers who brought morality to the "Wild West" while working at half the cost of a male's wage. This gave me my first sampling of the larger issues that emerge from education—gender, class, race, and other kinds of power divisions. I learned that mastering the intricacies of teaching go far beyond the "how tos" and techniques that characterize a functional and flowing classroom. They also include asking such questions as: Why am I teaching? Who decides what is taught? What impact will teaching have on the immediate and future lives of my students? What changes in my classroom will affect larger contexts, and in what directions? Asking these questions complicates an already very complex classroom practice. Nevertheless, these are crucial questions for my classroom's foundation; in order to effect my visions of a better world, I need to explore possible answers. This doesn't mean ignoring the wisdom of students, colleagues, parents, and so forth. Rather, it means, like the adventurous and struggling women teachers of 140 years ago, discovering what I believe democracy is and working to achieve it.

In my continued search, I have constructed five significant components that are essential to my understanding of democracy: personal meaning, ownership, cooperation and community, moral and ethical dimensions, and critical awareness. They serve as ideals on the basis of which I can build a just, democratic classroom.

Personal Meaning

The first component of my vision of democracy concerns the age-old search for life's meaning or purpose. What is meaningful for me? What do I strive for? When I wake up in the morning, what makes me want to jump out of bed? Discovering motivations in life can be a very empowering or a very scary experience. When I see my own motivations linked to actions that bear positive, productive fruit, my efforts are redoubled; this is empowering. However, when I learn that my actions hurt others or are no longer productive, I'm concerned that my foundation of ideals might collapse; this is scary. Through this process of success, failure, and reflective evaluation, meaning is found—and continues to be rediscovered—as I reach my goals, reprioritize, and learn. It is the same in classrooms: What is meaningful for me as a teacher, what is meaningful for each of my students, and what is meaningful for my community—classroom, school, and society—can be empowering.

Of course, it is difficult to quantify success in this component: How do I know if my teaching is worthwhile in the students' views? This reminds me of the classic teacher struggle to motivate students to read. I've seen all sorts of behavior modifications, self-esteem builders, and reading programs attempt to get students to read, but often enough the students don't want to read the assigned books.

The sixth graders I worked with during my internship with the Chicago Public Schools were not interested in reading *A Wrinkle in Time*, *The Lion, the Witch, and the Wardrobe*, *Harriet the Spy*, or many other books that are commonly considered classics of children's literature. For them and their lives, these books did not have significance or importance. Perhaps the backgrounds of the students didn't create a climate of interest in these books; or maybe they didn't build on the particular experiences of these students. In any event, I knew that the students weren't interested in these "classics" because they weren't being read even when assigned. So when I told the students they were to choose their own reading books (minus comic books) with some teacher assistance, they began a search for what was meaningful for them. Some students were ready for a variety of books; they chose mysteries, adventures, classics, or funny stories, and they read them all the way through. Others were more focused on their current story preferences and stuck to a certain genre of literature. Still other students groped around, choosing and discarding books until they found one that they were ready for—in terms of both reading level and plot. The students were enchanted by stories that reflected their own worlds and beliefs. The students, with teacher guidance, found their own interests and their own meanings.

Ownership

The second component of my democratic vision is a sense of genuine participation in or ownership of both daily and monumental decisions. Over what do I have power and control? How can I gain more control? Can I determine my own agenda and gauge my own influence? Who else is involved in this determination, and do I have some say in who they are? How do I communicate with others concerning this power and control? What sort of consequences does power-sharing have? What is the place of risk-taking in making decisions? Should personal risk be attached to decisions? How do decisions affect my desire to exercise responsibility? In any society, I have a right to be a significant participant in decision making and a profound contributor to the results of those decisions; thus, I engage in both reflection and action, the crux of praxis. There are opportunities, provided by both the society and me, to engage in dialogue over what is meaningful to the society and to me. As an extension of this dialogue, I can effect changes in my own life and those of others, sharing ownership of my life and the society in which I live.

The democratic classroom must include this opportunity for participation. Students, teachers, parents, and others involved in the educational effort are privy to information regarding changes and are able to influence the outcomes of those changes. With this power in hand, they can begin to actualize what they have found meaningful in life. Students can establish desk arrangements that suit them; teachers can demand parity in resource allocations; parents can be involved in textbook and literature choices. Of course, hand-in-hand with this power comes responsibility. The students, teachers, and parents have responsibilities for their decisions, whether they are risky and innovative or help maintain the status quo. An excellent example of ownership and responsibility was the school reform experiment in Chicago. Community members of various sorts—students, teachers, parents, and so forth—contributed to discussion, decision making, and program making in their schools. This reform provides one model of effective ownership of, power over, and input into a collective educational system.[1]

Cooperation and Community

The third component of my conception of empowered, democratic education is the development of cooperation and a sense of community. What format best fosters my sharing of power and decision making with others? What sort of bridge can I make with others who differ with my views? How can the tension between my ideals and existing social constraints be resolved without compromising principles? What sort of environment can be constructed so that I and others are collective owners of a decision and its enactment? I want very much to help make the world a better place; still, my perception of a better world might be inconsistent with another person's perception, even though it may have elements that are worth including. I might conclude, then, that an individualistic, isolationist tendency—that is, "every person for him/herself"—is an acceptable solution: All get what they want. However, this discounts the synergistic relationship among humans—the capacity to be so much more when working, thinking, and being with others. This isn't to discount the need for time alone or self-reflection but rather to emphasize the validity that cooperation generates, which in turn builds a living community.

The development of a community becomes especially crucial within the classroom, since it is a place where the individual and the larger group are often at odds: Who has power in what arena has a significant impact on classroom dynamics. If classroom members cannot arrive at negotiated agreements about issues, they will have a difficult time sharing power. Cooperation—among students, classrooms, and teachers—offers the mode by which this respectful and empathic negotiation can take place. The most obvious and simple example of this is who has control of the "podium"—that is, who is talking. At one time, I was playing "Capture the Flag" with a group of 6- to 12-year-old children in a summer day camp. While playing, almost all of our team members—including me—were captured. After waiting for some 10 minutes to be rescued, my "prisoner" teammates grew restless. They had screamed encouragement to our few remaining "free" team members to rescue us, but they would not come. They did not want to be captured too. Soon, the encouragement of the prisoners turned to threats and epithets. Mutiny and rebellion were suggested. Seeing that this could quickly get out of hand—that is, lose the cooperation of our team members and destroy the community of the game—I recommended to the prisoners that we hold a discussion in order to find a solution. Voices broke out immediately in a confused jumble, and no one could understand or follow a word. Without waiting for further chaos, I requested that we speak one at a time, so we could hear and be heard. The children agreed, and after a short, emotional rally, we united in declaring a forfeit for our team. Cooperation—being quiet, listening, and considering others' ideas— endured. Both in discussion and in activities, students encouraged and respected each other.

Moral and Ethical Dimensions

The fourth component of a democratic society involves moral and ethical dimensions of my and other people's thoughts and actions. What are my convictions? What do I think is right? How do I know it's right? How do I respond to or anticipate moral dilemmas? How do I perceive improv- ing this world? What gives me the authority to act on these perceptions? Though this might seem to be a somewhat nebulous component, I see it as an important contributor to discovering what is meaningful in life and buttressing that meaning with reasons. For me, finding or creating mean- ing is more than merely having direction or a goal to reach; it is having the inner strength and courage to confront social issues in my immediate life and surrounding environment. Moral frameworks provide the foundation on which this inner strength is based. They both prompt me to act when I see an apparent injustice and allow me to cherish that which is right.

As the history of schooling shows (Cremin, 1958; Kaufman, 1974), moral development has been a prominent goal of education and classroom life. Beyond legal attempts to remove religious practices from the school- house, and in spite of the efforts of the "religious Right" to establish prayer and other rituals as a permanent fixture of daily classroom life, moral val- ues and the teaching of morals are integrated into teaching and learning. The hidden curriculum and its emphasis on the values of diligence, punc- tuality, obedience, passivity, and so forth, certainly forge students' values and actions. My first full day of student teaching indicated to me that students and the classroom are profoundly affected by the moral structures of their environments.

There was already a bustle of students as I made my way to the overhead projector to put up the "Things to do" list for the prep period. As usual, my sixth graders did not sit down and read the board when they returned to class, but chatted or wandered around the room in search of excitement. Just as I was about to reach the overhead, I came across some excitement of my own. Out of the corner of my eye I saw two figures simultaneously shove each other. The culprits were Juan—a small, insecure Hispanic boy with a slight accent, and Darnell—a very active African-American boy with strong, well-developed interpersonal skills. The class hushed and time seemed to freeze. I took the lull in the action as an opportunity to lunge between the two of them, but I was slower than Darnell's right hook to Juan's jaw. In the crystal silence, the softest crunch of bone hitting bone could be heard. Juan paused as the punch's jolt reverberated through his body. The vibrations went down through his torso, arms, and legs only to bounce back up and into his head. His eyes flashed, and he threw himself at Darnell. Fortunately, I was in position to intercept him. Unfortunately, Juan would not give up until his attacker had been punished. "I'll kill him," he said. "I don't care what they do. I don't care if I'm suspended. I'll kill him." I physically restrained Juan for what seemed to be an eternity, finally driving him backward into the closet where the class could not see him give up his promised revenge.

We eventually worked out a resolution, but I was left with a sour taste in my mouth. What had happened? Why was Juan so intent on hurting Darnell? What sort of moral values were being communicated? What could the members of the school community have done to be more aware of those values and how to counteract them? Of course, I don't think Juan really would kill Darnell, but I do worry that his moral curriculum had taught him to believe that killing Darnell would be permissible. To me, it seemed as though his moral curriculum had amounted to little more than rejection and disrespect for his needs, two messages that had almost entirely devoured him. Without discussion, support, and challenge of his moral values, Juan had little hope to find meaning in his life or contributing significantly to his world.

Critical Awareness

The fifth component of an empowered citizenry is critical awareness and a willingness to challenge perceived authorities. *How* do I know? What tells me that I or someone else is right? What information helps me make the best decision? Who is benefitting from a decision? What are my and the group's agendas? What questions should I ask? By using powers of analysis to discern the difference between the real and the false, I am empowered to understand the dynamics that exist between myself and others. I can continuously reevaluate my and the group's convictions, so both might be strengthened in their reconstructions and additions. If, however, I were to weaken or fail to develop my critical consciousness, I would be stagnating morally, educationally, socially, and personally. To maintain my purpose in life, my participation in decision making, and my sense of community and convictions, I need to constantly share my perspectives with others and, in turn, listen to theirs. That is essential to growing and accepting criticism.

Here, too, the classroom provides one setting in which this component of a democratic society can be instantiated. In my classroom, students and teachers alike shared in the evaluation and reevaluation of their learning, perspectives, and power. For example, Johnny, a fifth grader, once challenged my choice of curricular themes: dinosaurs.

"What don't you like about dinosaurs?" I asked.

"They're boring, and I don't like writing," responded stolid, arms-crossed Johnny.

"Hmmmm, can you tell me more about your dislike of writing?"

"I don't like answering all those questions," he said, pointing to the list of "Dinosaur Discovery" questions.

I continued to encourage his rebellion, feeding him confidence that I hoped he would use constructively in the future. "What would you prefer to do, Johnny?" I put him on the spot.

Not thinking that he'd ever have to replace the curriculum with his own ideas, Johnny stared at me blankly and balked. "I dunno. Something else, like games outside."

Johnny seemed to feel he had lost the argument. He didn't have solid reasons for disliking dinosaurs, and he hadn't thought about a possible alternative. I told him this and encouraged him to give it more thought; then we could discuss his challenge again and perhaps design the next lesson together. This helped Johnny realize that he can have legitimate ideas that run counter to traditional authority—me, the teacher. And he can present those ideas with support from me. Johnny and I had enough trust that we were willing to offer sensitive insights and ask hard questions. Johnny learned about formulating his ideas, and I learned about Johnny's resistance to "dinosaur" activities. In this climate of cooperation, criticism was our teacher.

Personal meaning, ownership, cooperation and community, moral and ethical dimensions, and critical awareness are five principles that have guided my efforts to construct a democratic classroom. But by no means

do they lay out the entire substance of a democratic educational environment. Such an environment is far too complex and unpredictable to be
defined so formally, as the dynamism and interconnectedness of the
description of the components displayed. Democratic education is continuously evolving and its components are tightly interwoven, an indication
of the close relationship between school and society and the larger issues
this relationship entails.

IMPEDIMENTS TO A DEMOCRATIC CLASSROOM

While ideals have given me the conceptual framework with which I
hope to construct my classroom, it has been the misplanned activities and
lesson "mistrials" that have shown me what can derail or disrupt a democratic classroom. As a teacher who devises classroom structures, I look for
the educational misgivings and faults, so I might avoid them or eradicate
them from my practice. As a result of my experiences, I have found three
particularly difficult issues that play havoc with my attempts to democratize education: student interest versus curricular imposition; classroom
management and control; and the lack of opportunity to reflect and plan.

What Susie and Deborah Want to Do:
Student Interest Versus Curricular Imposition

What does the student want to learn? What do I, the teacher, want
students to learn? The amount of overlap between these two questions is
the extent to which the student and I agree on classroom organization and
the content of the curriculum. In an empowering setting, the learner certainly has an important contribution to make to decisions regarding subject matter, just as I, the teacher, do. What happens when the overlap
between these two questions is minimal or nonexistent? What sort of
power-sharing is acceptable and fair? Do I as the teacher have more right
or responsibility to impose what I believe to be an acceptable and fair
curriculum? Or does the student, as the active learner, have more right to
select the material? How do we reach an accord on this?

I once served as the Learning Coordinator at a summer day camp,
where I restructured a traditional, small-group tutoring program into theme-
based, whole-group educational activities. Whereas the original, traditional
program served 1–4 students at a time for 2 half-hour sessions each week,
the new program consisted of weekly themes and daily, hour-long sessions.
Thus, each child received much more attention and learned more, though
in a larger group. But not everyone liked the new design. Several students

approached me about the change in format. They asked me why we couldn't go back to the old system where they could do what they wanted and not follow the camp's weekly theme.

"Erin, we want to go back to the old way," complained Susie, a short fifth grader who was not shy about expressing her point of view.

Chipped in her friend Deborah, "Yeah, we don't like this dinosaur stuff. It's too hard."

She was referring to an activity where she found her own weight, the weight of a dinosaur, and how many of her equaled one dinosaur, an exercise in division and comparison. Another friend of theirs joined in the fray, and the dissent appeared to be growing. The activities weren't beyond their capabilities, but they still weren't interested. What was I to do? I wanted to encourage dissension and critical reflection; after all, they are key parts of a democratic classroom. Shouldn't I even encourage them to develop their own ideas and themes? Yet I couldn't possibly prepare 80 different themes each week, and I wouldn't allow them to walk all over what I thought were exciting lessons. Many other children had given me positive feedback, so I was quite content with the design of the lesson. I thought of my options. Should I change the entire theme to accommodate them? Allow them to spin off their own projects, where they could learn at their own pace, utilizing their own interests? Impose on them my authority to do what I thought best for them? None of these seemed to exemplify the model democratic classroom; they all swung too far to one side, mine or theirs. So I thought of using the instance as a lesson in itself. I encouraged them to critique the lesson.

I asked them questions like: "What don't you like about the new format?" "What did you like about the old way?" "What would you like to see changed?" "What do I need to do?"

They mostly stumbled as they searched for reasons to support their dislike of the system and couldn't give any reason for the former system. As we rounded out the conversation, they were still whining somewhat, but they seemed to realize the weakness of their cause. Still, I felt that, in my meager attempt to be democratic, I had been somewhat heavy-handed in my attempt to persuade them. Was I overusing my authority to impose my views on Susie and Deborah? How much input into their curriculum did they have? What level of participation did I permit?

I'm not sure of the answers to these questions. Somewhere in each instance of imposition, there is probably an appropriate amount of teacher and student decision making. Susie, Deborah, and I discovered that amount only as we were engaged in discussion; it wasn't something we could know beforehand. Despite the possibility of being too heavy-handed, it was crucial that Susie and Deborah learn decision-making skills, moral values, and cooperation through the process of negotiation. A democratic classroom lives democracy, giving Susie and Deborah the power to make decisions and to ride and fall on those decisions, to learn from and be responsible for those decisions. It is not a contrived situation of playful, academic exercises for the self-effacing or the shy.

Bridget's Rocks: Classroom Management and Control

Many times I am struck by my intense desire to control an activity, to fashion it into what parents, administrators, and I call "model learning." I want a lesson to be truly a learning experience; I want the children, whatever they're doing, to be safe and secure while they nod their absorbing heads. Yet I must stop children who are running haphazardly through an art project, wrestling without regard to the sharp desk corners, or carrying scissors like a sword. In the complex and distracting environment of the classroom, I feel often as if I must pointedly intervene. This means maintaining discipline. It means setting hard, clear, and sometimes impersonal parameters and expectations, so students know the acceptable limitations. Only then do the students know exactly where to—and where not to—tread. In other words, I'm looking for some way to create an order within the chaos of democratic learning. Is this possible? Is there such an order? How do I define it? What sort of chaos is valid for the students, the community (parents, administrators, and other teachers), and me? Do behavioristic rewards and punishments have merit in teaching a child how to develop common sense—for example, that screaming epithets at another child in a public (or private) place is simply not acceptable behavior? Or am I sacrificing democratic ideals for the authoritarian path of safety and ease? Once I had a conversation with a little girl named Bridget, who convinced me that I must continually pay attention to this issue.

As we came inside from recess, six-year-old Bridget, as usual, lazily brought up the rear. I waited patiently, for two reasons: I knew she enjoyed exploring the world and appreciating everything that passed by, and I had been tipped off that Bridget had hidden rocks in her shoes. Feeling as though I needed to gently confront Bridget for attempting to smuggle rocks into the building, I paused at the door and asked her if she had rocks in her shoes. She looked up slowly, the guilt clearly on her face.

"Yes," she replied.

"Would you please take them out? We can't have rocks in the building," I said in my most tolerant voice. But she wouldn't settle for my authority; she apparently liked those rocks.

As she began taking off her shoes and pulling out her tiny rocks she asked, "Why?"

I was dumbfounded. Internally, I asked myself the same question. Why? Why did I need to exercise my power to remove the rocks from her shoes? What was it going to do to Bridget, her learning, or her environment? Something hurtful? Wasn't she developing an aesthetic appreciation, perhaps one that I should corroborate?

"Well, Bridget, that's a very good question," I said. "I'm not sure how to answer that."

She waited patiently, all the while commenting on the prettiness of her three little stones and pointing out the stripes and colorful patterns. I knelt down beside Bridget and told her, "Bridget, you're right. You like those rocks. But I'm concerned that they might hurt your feet if you leave them in your shoes. In the future, please don't put them there. You can take these stones inside. You found some very pretty ones."

We talked for a moment or so about the rocks, and then she gathered them up and we joined the others inside.

In Bridget's case, I felt an immediate necessity to impose my power over her, to tell her what was acceptable and unacceptable, to give her clear, uncompromising direction. But was that fair? Was that democratic? Was Bridget controlling her situation and living by her own decision to take her rocks inside? How much of an environment of tolerance, respect, and empathy was I building? While I was superficially cooperative, my deeper motive was to control Bridget and her intentions. It was her questioning that stimulated our exploration of the issue at hand. In fact, as I look back, there are scores of lessons that could be derived from that little incident. There are issues of property—who owns those rocks? issues of geology— how are those pretty patterns created? issues of aesthetics—what makes those rocks pretty? issues of responsibility—can anything be brought into the classroom from outside? and lots more to play with. I was very happy to see that both Bridget and I had learned that we can challenge authorities, respectfully engage in dialogue, and act on the convictions we build from that dialogue. Bridget kept her rocks and her curiosity from being taken away by me, and I obtained the ability to take a risk by trusting a child to have substantial reasons.

When Can I Think?
Opportunities to Reflect and Plan

I have learned that as democratic life is much more than the isolated act of voting, so democratic education is more than momentary action. Democracy is both reflection *and* action—in one word, praxis. As my classroom experiences have sometimes molded themselves around this concept, reflection grows out of action, action grows out of reflection, and the two become intricately intertwined. But mundane teaching tasks and the need to comply with external forces devour my time for praxis. It is hard for me to think about gender issues or personal empowerment as I'm filling out daily attendance forms or setting up lab equipment. There isn't much time for my students to discuss classroom rules or fair desk arrangements when we are concentrating on covering grammar rules for their upcoming Iowa Test of Basic Skills. Do I maintain the status quo, so my class might do well on these tests? Textbooks and curriculum guides could easily think for me; most everything is laid out already. But then teaching becomes following a recipe; I read it once for the gist, twice for clarity, and succumb to its impersonality, rigidity, and hierarchical origins. This destroys my democratic convictions, which I'm unwilling to do. Perhaps, then, I build in time for serious reflection and let the students' multiplication tables or phonics suffer. But I don't want to create an idyllic world that is isolated from real life. That would be a disservice to my students; they would be unprepared for what *their* democratic lives entail. Also, the realities of my job and career could be on the line. How do I respond to a parent or a school board member who complains that the curriculum serves no tangible or appropriate purpose? Maybe our problem-posing and critical investigations can provide the math and reading comprehension skills that standardized tests and subsequent grades require. Is there a happy medium, where both worlds can be accommodated? *Should* I accommodate both worlds? The need for reflective and active experiences is vital, but controlled trade-offs seem to be the only answer.

The typical day for me during my Chicago Public School internship was to prepare for the day, teach, meet with other teachers to prepare, and evaluate student work. There was no time to think! The only moments for reflection were on the way to or returning from school and in short snatches while planning with other teachers. As a result, my wonderings and concerns about curricular adjustments, individual students, and creating a democratic classroom went by the wayside. I wondered how I could restructure my day so I could at least spend some time considering the impact of my democratic principles on my classroom.

Though I never had a time in which I thoroughly analyzed and evaluated everything I had experienced in each day's classroom, I was able to reflect in a journal twice a week and initiate conversations and request advice from veteran teachers I traveled with to and from school. This helped solidify my democratic vision. Still, I had many unanswered questions and dissatisfactions left from these conversations and writings. I think a supportive, like-minded group of teachers, meeting on a regular, frequent basis, would have provided further strength to my reflections and actions.

INITIATING THE DEMOCRATIC CLASSROOM

My experiences, and my principles for a democratic classroom, provided two important reminders to me. One, the youngest children—even eight- and nine-year-old, non-native English speakers—can have valid and important points of view to express to those in power. They, too, can act as teachers, even to those who are called teachers—the principal, the bus driver, my cooperating teacher, and me. The student and the teacher coexist as both learners and teachers, not as isolated identities.

Furthermore, like the young students teaching the teachers, inexperienced teachers have much to offer those with more experience. The enthusiasm of new teachers for supposedly naive ideals is an important part of continuing to reexamine the philosophies and practices that have been around for so long. With higher education's "ivory tower" in my recent past, I have the responsibility to share my educational dreams and hopes for a better classroom, a better world. No matter the age or position, the language spoken, or the degrees conferred, all can learn from others. It is in this respectful, open interchange that democratic classrooms, and ultimately a democratic way of life, are built.

NOTE

1. For some information on these reforms, see Simmons, 1992; and *Catalyst: Voices of Chicago School Reform*, copies of which are available through the Community Renewal Society, 332 S. Michigan Avenue, Chicago, IL 60604.

REFERENCES

Cremin, L. A. (1958). *The republic and the school: Horace Mann on the education of free men*. New York: Teachers College Press.
Kaufman, P. W. (1974). *Women teachers on the frontier*. New Haven: Yale University Press.
Roche, E. (1991). *Differences and contrasts between the educational ideals of Horace Mann and the experiences of women teachers on the frontier*. Unpublished paper written for Educational Studies 202, History of Education, Knox College.
Simmons, A. (1992, August 11). School reform—success story or noble failure: Proof of progress in the classroom. *Chicago Tribune*, p. 17.

THREE

Creating Space:
Moving from the Mandatory
to the Worthwhile

Ushma Shah

Teaching, like poetry, involves insight, imagination, creativity, struggle, and sometimes frustration: How can I capture the image, the beauty, the form? What symbols can I utilize, what metaphors can I invent? What meanings might I convey, what reflections can I foster? Perhaps the intensity, emotion, and drama of teaching can themselves best be captured in poetic form. Or at any rate perhaps my own poem may provide an introduction to how I think and feel about teaching.

Teaching

Rising through
urgent streaks of
Faber-Castell fluorescent:
her words:

> "The whole exercise of creative writing, the reaching back into the mind for something to say, nurtures the organic idea and exercises the inner eye" (Ashton-Warner, 1963, p. 55).

his words:

> "Democracy and democratic education are founded on faith in men, on the belief that they not only can but should discuss the problems of their country, of their continent, their world, their work, the problems of democracy itself. Education is an act of love, and thus an act of courage" (Freire, 1990, p. 38).

---

and her words:

> "What are the words you do not yet have? What do you need to say?
> What are the tyrannies you swallow day by day and attempt to make
> your own, until you will sicken and die of them, still in silence? Perhaps
> for some of you here today, I am the face of one of your fears. Because
> I am woman, because I am Black, because I am lesbian, because I am
> myself—a Black woman warrior poet doing my work—come to ask
> you, are you doing yours?" (Lorde, 1977)

echo, ricochet
dream scream
inside books
arranged by size on my shelf.
Outside, as I move through everyday, around heavy requirements and over
large assumptions, these are some of the voices that undergird my day.

Skimming the bindings
I revisit
themes, images, quotes, notes, passion, discussions
Reaching across the space, the space between
these books, these words
and
the point on which I stand
are possibilities undefined but directed
shapeless and marching.

This is where it happens. I look around for my friends. Take my pencil and
my mind. Walk in that direction. This is where it happens. The making of
visions. . . .

When family or friends of my family ask me what I majored in at Knox
College or what I want to do in the future, I know I am usually in for an
interesting conversation. I majored in educational studies and sociology/
anthropology. While certain family acquaintances and most of my friends
are supportive of my teaching and my inquiry into non-technical, non-
lucrative disciplines, others react in simultaneously humorous and disturbing ways. On hearing of my plans to teach at the elementary school level,
for example, one of my uncles some time ago asked, "What happened? You
did not score well on the SAT?" A neighbor simply replied, "Oh ho, what
boring subjects!" And one of my aunts, concerned for my parents, asked,
"But your sister is studying to be a mechanical engineer, right?"

My decision to become a teacher was not based in bad SAT scores,
bad advising, or bad karma. My decision to become a teacher emerged from

hope for a just world and broader commitments to democracy, equality, and social change.

FORMING COMMITMENTS: WHERE I AM COMING FROM

If who we are tells something about where we have been, then how we teach tells something about where we want to go.

I have memories of myself as an elementary school student trying to hide my Indianness, telling my mother I would not go to the store with her until she took her *bindi* off, being embarrassed when my grandparents wore traditional clothing and stood in our yard, wanting to be "normal." Whenever I was angry or frustrated about these feelings of embarrassment, I kept them as secrets between me and my diary, sometimes between me and my sister. Later, in high school, I had some friends and some experiences that made me challenge this view of myself, of my culture. I began writing thoughts, expressions, and ideas down more consciously in the form of poems, stories, and images. This act of reflecting on how and why I was always wanting to hide part of myself and expressing those thoughts through writing and visual images began my thinking about how my schooling experiences could have been better, about what should have been different.

Without being certain what it was I wanted to do, I enrolled in a college liberal arts program and walked into a process of awareness. Through readings, discussions, and experiences that made me confront my own world view, I became conscious of issues of class, race, sex, and privilege that previously flowed underneath and untouched by my everyday concerns. Issues of classism were highlighted when I began to see the distinct physical and psychological separation between the students, faculty, administrators, and office personnel of my private college and the people who kept the grounds, cleaned our dorms, made our food; of the way these employees were generally not included in the common campus reference to "our community." I saw the constant, enraging pattern of "men who talk" and "women who work" at family gatherings, community functions, and even in certain circles of friends. As part of these images, I realized the dichotomies with which I viewed the world: male/female, homosexual/ heterosexual, rich/poor, good/bad, and the oppression inherent in looking at the world this way. As I was involved in observing public schools, I began to understand and resent the inequality of school funding—the undemocratic way in which suburban taxes paid for my privileged education while many of my peers in city schools were victims of old facilities and little money. Listening carefully to the mainstream news, I recognized how we are bombarded by the justification of sexist, racist, and exploit-ative paradigms: the twisted broadcasts of the United States in Grenada, Guatemala, and the Persian Gulf.

With this process of becoming conscious of the racism, sexism, and classism in my life came the exploration of how these examples related to the larger picture, the broader global patterns. That is, I began to under-stand that issues of race, class, and gender did not exist isolated from other discussions but overlapped and reinforced each other. All of this was about the demystification of the world, the feeling that I have the capability and the responsibility to understand, interpret, and change my worlds.

But any amount of realization, anger, consciousness, and becoming meant nothing if it happened in the isolation of my mind, in my small sphere of existence. The words and reflection were hollow without action. *Praxis.* I began to seek ways to act, to make these ideas move outside my mind and into shared life.

Working with friends and campus organizations to confront and address controversial issues of "political correctness," student voice, and the CIA, I learned the importance of interrogating common perspectives and of challenging paradigms. Tutoring high school students and working with adults through the Heartland Literacy Coalition, I learned the power of teaching, the empowerment of teaching. One of the adult students, Oliver, and I decided that instead of working with the basic curriculum supplied by the literacy program, we would read material that we felt was more important, such as "real" newspaper articles, old letters from his daughter, and flyers he received in the mail. At this time, I was reading Dewey's (1902/1956) *The Child and the Curriculum* and Freire's (1992) *Pedagogy of the Oppressed* in an education course. I began to notice par-allels between the issues and perspectives in the readings and the time I spent with Oliver, the integration of the theory I studied and the moment of working with Oliver.

In this way, I began to think about how teaching moves toward action and liberation, about how my developing social vision can be animated through teaching that works toward democracy, equality, and social change. Although I was not and am not able to talk about a utopia in a completely comprehensive way, I know my social vision is about a place that is not like what exists here, now:

> We become submerged in meaninglessness and believe that this is all there is when really we are not breathing until we believe that there is more, until we let ourselves feel and see humanness and become conscious of false conceptions that some people deserve more than others, that equality and democracy are simply the right to check a name on the ballot, that we live

and can be understood out of our contexts, that the world is simple, linear, and just. Perhaps we are not thinking until we reflect and reflect again, until we look for ways to penetrate the meaningless and find ourselves moving toward what we want, moving toward a world in which we are aware of who we are, the communities we belong to, the world dimensions where there is no political system separate from a social system—only a world in which all of these possibilities swirl together, overlap and interconnect to splash lives bursting with life, direction, equality and humanness. (Shah, 1991)

THE REALITY QUESTION

As my peers and I began to read, think about, and discuss our commitments to justice and equality, and how they would inform what and how we teach, and as I began to value the time I spent tutoring Oliver, I understood that what I wanted students to experience was the kind of awareness that I had experienced through readings, discussions, friends, and experiences—the empowerment not only to see the world but to envision possibility and change.

But the question remained: What would this mean in the reality of teaching: to the lesson plans, the homework, the dissected days, and the diverse interests? During my student teaching semester, I struggled to mesh worthwhile experiences with the often mundane objectives that had to be taught, to do things that were different without putting off my cooperating teacher and school administrators whose perceptions were tied to the possibilities of my student teaching.

Student Teaching: The Scene

I completed student teaching through the Urban Education Program (UEP) sponsored by the Associated Colleges of the Midwest. Although many prospective teachers do student teaching at schools near their colleges, through the UEP, educational studies students at any of the 14 consortium schools from Minnesota to Colorado can apply to complete their student teaching while living in Chicago.

I was placed in a fifth-grade "gifted" classroom at South Elementary School, an ethnically and economically diverse school. The 588 member student body was 17.6% white, 35.9% African-American, 42.9% Latino, 3.6% Asian, and 0% Native American.[1] Part of the desegregation process, the gifted classrooms were meant to attract students from wealthier areas and included white, African-American, and Asian students. The non-gifted classrooms, cleverly referred to as "neighborhood classrooms," consisted of mainly African-American students.

The structure and routine of South would not be foreign to anyone familiar with the workings of the typical Chicago public school. Teachers signed in at the office each morning and collected lunch tickets and announcements from their mailboxes. The students waited outside until the bell rang at 8:50 AM. The day began with the "Pledge of Allegiance" and the "Star-Spangled Banner" over the intercom, a brief message from the principal, a recitation of the lunch menu, and special announcements. Twice a week, each class had library and gym class. There was a teacher cafeteria and a student cafeteria. Teachers, however, were required to monitor their classes during the lunch break and therefore sat in the student lunch room. There were teacher rest rooms and student rest rooms. The student rest rooms usually had no toilet paper.

Testing was central to the South routine. In addition to the week-long standardized exams (such as the Illinois Goals Assessment Plan [IGAP], the Iowa Test of Basic Skills, and teachers' regular chapter/unit tests), South also administered schoolwide standardized math and reading progress exams at the end of each month. The tests were ready-made and were included as part of the curriculum. Each classroom teacher would give the test to his or her class and then bring the Scantron answer sheets to the office in a brown folder labeled "March Math Exam, Room 206," "June Reading Test, Room 304," and so forth. The following week the brown folders would reappear in the teachers' mailboxes. Enclosed would be the electronically graded answer sheets and a satin ribbon for each student who scored above 95% on a test. Teachers would then bring these folders back to the class to record scores in the grade book, to tell students how they had done, and to announce who received ribbons. This announcement, however, fluctuated little from month to month; some students usually got ribbons, others usually didn't.

It is in the setting of this community and this school that I taught in Room 207. The students in my fifth-grade classroom were encouraging, diverse, and very lively. My cooperating teacher, Cindy Tenner, a young and enthusiastic teacher who supported me and was willing to let me experiment with new methods of teaching, was central to the success of my student teaching semester. Additionally, I had a UEP advisor who was constantly offering resources, suggestions, and support during the semester.

Room 207 was well lit, with windows along one entire wall. The other walls were part of the standard public school environment: chalkboards, bulletin boards, a teacher closet, and student closets. Instead of rows of desks with the teacher desk at the helm, Cindy had organized the room in pods of six desks each. The six students in each group gave themselves a name and would work together during cooperative activities or to collect resources for projects, field trips, and so forth. There was one computer at the back of the classroom. Two to four students worked on the computer for approximately 20 minutes each morning while Cindy was dealing with attendance, lunch money, and other morning tasks. During this morning organization period, other students were to quietly work on the assignment on the board or to prepare for the current events discussion. It is during this period that the principal's voice would come over the intercom and the day would officially begin.

Prepackaged Curriculum and Pre-given Objectives: First Insights into Teacher Limitations

Voluntarily orchestrating whole-class performances and dramatic readings of African-American poetry for school assemblies, encouraging interviews of women family members and studies of women in history, Cindy was dedicated to moving beyond what was required of teachers at South. At the same time, she was always making sure that she was teaching the mandated objectives outlined in school curriculum guidelines and the objectives stated before each lesson in the social studies, math, science, reading, and spelling textbooks. After all, the machines that would eventually evaluate her own teaching and her students' knowledge through standardized IGAP tests would only sense the marks of a number-2 pencil; they would not hear students singing and performing pieces of African-American history. The mandated objectives were one of the first lenses through which I began to understand how teachers' power is limited and how our positions are deskilled and devalued.

As my cooperating teacher, Cindy was certain to stress the importance of including and teaching the stated objectives. She told me that I could teach the objectives in different ways: through the lesson plans given in the teachers' manuals, lectures, worksheets, group activities, or projects. However, the "Students will be able to . . . " statements at the beginning of each lesson in the teacher's manuals were to guide my curriculum. At the end of the lesson, the pre-given objectives must be met; to ignore these objectives was to jeopardize important test scores.

From the first day of my student teaching and this first conversation with Cindy about objectives and planning lessons, I began to understand the creativity needed to maneuver between the extremely specific, predetermined objectives that had to be taught and the experiential and empowering education that I would call worthwhile. Two examples illustrate this maneuvering.

I was to teach the next reading lesson in the text. The title of the lesson was "Visualizing as an Aid in Getting Meaning" (Explorations, 1986, p. 156). The expected procedure for teaching this objective was to read three excerpts from the teachers' manual and ask the students to describe the pictures they saw in their minds. The excerpts were not connected to anything else in the curriculum, nor were they connected to each other. That is, one passage was a descriptive paragraph about a man who trips while walking his dog, another was about two friends baking in the kitchen, and so forth. The students were then to complete a workbook page related to visualizing skills. This format, the recommended and sometimes enforced way to teach a particular reading skill, was bland and one-dimensional.

Since Cindy was not a traditional teacher and I could teach the objectives in any way I wanted, I decided to use a variety of Native American legends that would tie into the "Earth" theme that Cindy, another teacher, and I had cooperatively selected. Instead of completing meaningless and alienating workbook pages, students read three Native American legends: "How Grandmother Spider Stole the Sun" (Creek), "Creation of the Animal People" (Okanogan), and "White Buffalo Woman" (Sioux). Then, as a class, we described the pictures that the legends provoked in our minds, and discussed the concept of imagery and how these pieces tied into our "Earth" theme: "What pictures do these legends give you? What colors do you imagine? Did anyone see anything different? How do the people who created this legend feel about the Earth? What makes you believe this?" Students then illustrated the legends and shared their drawings with the class. We discussed how these legends related to the creative stories we had written using garbage collected during our playground cleanup initiative, and whether any of the material learned from these legends could help us plan the "skits about the Earth" we were going to perform at the next school assembly. In this way, the lesson had a context and was connected to other issues, topics, and images of our learning.

I felt confident about the way I had taught the visualizing lesson and that the method I used was better than the one "prescribed" by the text because visualizing the Native American legends moved toward affective and artistic learning and away from alienating workbooks. However, would I be able to repeat this process of teaching text objectives in creative ways in other cases? In all cases?

Later, in the middle of my internship, the class was completing Chapter 5 in the reading text. This took place during the Rodney King beating, trial injustices, and the Los Angeles riots. Since the issues surrounding the trial and the riots were important to students in the morning "Current Events" discussion and central to the conversations, debates, and actions taking place in the country, I searched for ways to integrate the Rodney King issues with the objectives and flow of the class.

I was constrained by limited time and the pressure to teach chapters efficiently. And since I could not find a way to connect these issues with objectives of the current social studies, math, science, or reading chapters, I skipped to the objective of the Chapter 7 reading lesson, which aimed to teach students the difference between fact and opinion. I taught this Chapter 7 objective through different newspaper articles about the Rodney King beatings, the trial, and the Los Angeles riots, which we read, discussed, debated, and then analyzed for fact and opinion: "Is this headline a fact or an opinion? What about this quotation? What makes an opinion? What makes a fact? Some people say that there is no such thing as a 'fact.' What might they mean? Why is a court ruling a fact? Isn't it just a decision based upon different opinions? Aren't the laws of courts based on opinions?"

Teaching this way, I hope, meant inciting students to listen carefully to the news they heard, to question the assumptions they had about the court system, and to be critical of the way they understood this moment. Teaching this way, however, also meant breaking the reading lesson sequence—jumping from the objectives of Chapter 5 to those of Chapter 7—and jeopardizing students' test scores if I did not "cover" the material I had skipped before the next standardized exam. Because I was a student teacher and because Cindy had clearly advised me to teach the objectives, I made sure that although I had created space to include the Rodney King issues in the curriculum, I went back and taught the lessons that would be covered on the next monthly exam.

While I was a student teacher, it was not the fact of having "objectives" that bothered me, but the fact that they came from the outside and predetermined the specific reactions of each student to each lesson. The more specific, quantified, and dissected these pre-given objectives were, the less leeway I had in interpreting them and planning my lessons. In addition, and most importantly, extremely narrow and focused objectives limited students to uniform responses and detracted from their creativity. The focused objectives implied that every student should see this reading in this way or that math problem in that way. If a school curriculum guide stated, instead, that an objective to be met at the fifth-grade level was to "explore the fundamentals of chemistry," space would be left for lessons to emerge from students' interests, to include creative endeavors, to connect the teaching of this objective with other ideas in the class. But, in terms of allowing teachers to develop as curriculum designers, in terms of varied student interests, cultural differences, range of learning styles, and the changing context from classroom to classroom, "Students will be able to recite the noble gases, define their characteristics and identify their location on the periodic table" is not a malleable or necessarily relevant objective.

In the context of the complex social, political, and economic world in which we claim to be preparing students to live, simplistic conceptions of education as universal lists of "things to know" must be challenged. We have to think about ways to make school have meaning, ways for education to be relevant to students' perspectives, culture, time, and place. A regurgitation model of education runs counter to students' empowerment and the re-creation of democracy because it essentially mutes student interests, intelligence, desires, and initiatives. If we are serious about creating classrooms and schools that teach students to exercise democracy, to live and act responsibly, then we must move from the scientific and technical language of "students will be able to recite X and define Y" to a more open and exploratory conception of education that allows students to experiment, critique, challenge, search, define and redefine, create, and act in an organic way.

Throughout the texts in my classroom, there was evidence of a spoon-feeding attitude toward learning and teaching. The prescribed texts and their stated objectives were not based on an interest in making sure that the students are engaged and actively participating in the curriculum, only that certain bits of information are transmitted to their minds. In this sense, most of the material lacked substance and was based in narrow, technical thought as opposed to mind-broadening activities and challenging ideas.

Deskilled: The Teacher as Puppet

In addition to limiting students and teachers in the ways discussed, the prescribed curriculum in my fifth-grade class was devaluing of teacher intelligence and oftentimes insulting. Outlining a linear route through each of the units, the Teacher's Edition of these texts was specific and direct, rigid and condescending.

While doing a curriculum analysis as part of my undergraduate work, I looked closely at a primary reading curriculum. This curriculum shared many important similarities with the typical textbook at South. Containing a step-by-step guide of how to proceed through each phase of "Teaching the Lesson," the Teacher's Edition contained revealing and patronizing language. I remember that at one point it instructed the teacher, for example, to "Tell students to recite what they learned in this chapter. Use the following questions: (1) . . . " and "Respond to specific questions with appropriate answers," and finally, "Dictate the following instructions, sentences, and stories." All of these commands are explicitly defined and leave no room for innovation. The curriculum is complete and objectified to the point that input from the teacher would seem out of place, a curve in the scientific, straight lines of this curriculum made by people who "know what they are talking about."

If most of the texts in my classroom were used in the prescribed ways, the interactions between teacher and students would be one-dimensional, surface-level, relatively passive, and constantly under the curriculum designers' control. Teachers and students would be going through the motions, reading and answering the workbook questions, but there would be no controversy, no driving questions, no passion. If most of this curriculum was used in the way it was intended, there would be no movement toward the unity of community, no sense of what it is to be critically conscious of who we are and what is going on around us, no feeling of being part of a democracy.

The material learned would exist outside of the student and have no connection to his or her realities, to the worlds that he or she will face after graduating, after this grade level, or after school on that particular day. The knowledge learned through these workbook pages, banal readings, and usually trivial textbook activities would not be powerful; it would not urge the students to ask *why* their community is falling apart while other communities have large, growing businesses and opportunities; *why* all of the honorable people in their history books are from one part of the world when the world they see everyday is filled with people from different places, of different colors; or *why*, if we have a Constitution that grants freedom to speak out, students in schools are told constantly to shut up, sit down, raise their hand, speak when called on, and not to question the decisions of the teacher.[2]

Thus, embedded in the prescribed texts and the teachers' manuals was, first, the view of the student as an object, not a fellow human being to be respected or an individual capable and worthy of depth and dialogue; and second, a patronizing attitude conveying the view that unless every step is laid out, teachers will not be capable of acting in the interests of their students.

Throughout the term I had a feeling of being trapped between packaged objectives and the search for ways to implement a worthwhile curriculum, one that would value controversy and instigate thought in the classroom. I also struggled to assert my understanding that a teacher is a curriculum designer and not a mere conveyer of someone else's information. This was the process of "creating space" between the tension of teaching the mandatory and implementing the worthwhile.

"CREATING SPACE": MOVING TOWARD THE WORTHWHILE

The gifted fifth-grade social studies text covered world history. When I began my student teaching term, the class was just beginning the unit on

Islam. Again, I was required to teach the stated objectives but could approach them from any angle. The textbook portrayal of Islam focused on the "spreading of Islam" and the acquisition of territory. Therefore, the stated objectives included: "Students will be able to: 1) explain why Muslims fought for Islam; 2) locate the boundaries of the Islamic Empire; 3) explain how Islam continued to spread" (*World Past to Present*, 1989, p. 114).

Teaching little about Muslim culture, people, the differences between Shiite or Sunni, beliefs in Sharia law or *zakat*, the chapter focused on conquered land and the triumphs and defeats of selected caliphs. The views, diversity, and current lives of Muslims, the book covertly teaches, are less relevant than the image of Muslims as people who live in arid areas and are most important for having a history of acquiring land through war—a misconception that meshes nicely with media misrepresentations of Muslims. In this way, the world history text illustrated a clear example of biased and stereotype-perpetuating curriculum. Becoming conscious of this slant in the telling of history and in the telling of all stories is integral to viewing the world in a critical and empowering way. Since I myself was struggling with the narrow nature of the curriculum texts, I decided to use this Islam chapter as a launching point for students to begin to critique their own texts.

Students were asked to read an article entitled "Blacks Only One Group Ignored in History Class," by Jennifer Thompson (1992), from *New Expressions*, a newspaper published by Chicago public school students. We then worked in "Think, Pair, Share" cooperative learning groups to discuss: "Was the writer of this article from *New Expressions* off-base? Is it possible that our history books are inaccurate? Why would this be? Is everything in our history books 'true' or 'fair?'" In an active discussion about these questions, students approached critical issues regarding differences in perspective, the meaning of "the truth" when people have different understandings of an event, and the reasons some groups may be left out of or unfairly portrayed in, in this case, our history books. Students were asked to keep these ideas in mind as we proceeded through the Islam unit.

During our one-week study of Islam, we touched on all the objectives mandated by the text; this was mainly accomplished through extrinsic lecture and question/answer format classroom dynamics. We also supplemented the book with mapmaking, excerpts from the Koran, presentations from the two Muslim students in our class, and a detailed exploration of the five pillars of Islam through cooperative learning groups.

Then, before closing the chapter, we went back to our original discussion about history books and the idea that if we had learned only from the text, we might have gotten a slanted perspective on Islam. Students pointed out how much more they learned from Issac and Aliya, the two

Muslim students, and their sharing of experiences, knowledge, and artifacts. We looked at the illustrations in the text and talked about what impressions they gave us about Muslim people, about the Middle East, and about women in this region. I showed the class 10 to 12 college-level books on different aspects of Islam. As they looked through the pictures of Islamic-influenced architecture and the Kaaba, and as they flipped through books and essays about Islam, social change, and Muslim women, we talked about the concept of summarizing: "If the history text covered Islam in less than 10 pages and here we were looking at hundreds of pages about different aspects of Islam, what has been left out? Who made these decisions? Are there any topics covered in these books that were left out of the text? What are some examples?"

Through these interactions and the dynamics of these discussions, our class moved toward a community of dialogue in which we listened, debated, and challenged. While the teachers' manual suggested simple and narrow methods—"Ask students to explain why Muhammed was puzzled by the religious beliefs of Jews and Christians. . . . Then have students write a paragraph in which they explain . . . " (*World Past to Present*, 1989, p. 120)—we had moved beyond these parameters and into a deeper, more ethical, and more vivid understanding of history and of Islam.

The more our discussions incited passion, sincere questions, and challenging ideas, the closer and more genuine our conversations and experiences became. This sense of community developed through subsequent units, activities, projects, and discussions that focused on the power of triggering interest and emotion, such as the Columbus children's book critique activity in which students analyzed the biased portrayal of a powerful and intelligent Columbus and the negatively and stereotypically portrayed Native Americans in several children's books (Bigelow, 1991). Using this knowledge, students were then encouraged to write and illustrate their own children's books, which could teach younger children about Columbus in a more accurate and ethical way. And in the Mohen-jo-daro projects that made the students in our class into archaeologists, students worked in groups to study the Mohen-jo-daro excavation sites, created an archaeological discovery, wrote a paper on their discovery using archaeological terminology and the Mohen-jo-daro context, and presented their findings at the "International Archeology Conference" that we hosted in our classroom.

Developing and facilitating these lessons began to focus my understanding of words such as "student-centered learning," "empowerment," and "intrinsic motivation" and what these ideas looked like in the three dimensions of a real classroom. While the feeling in my classroom was open and encouraging from the beginning, Cindy also commented on a difference in the way students were engaged in the content of our work and drawn into our discussions in new ways. These moments of interest and intensity entered class discussions and posed new questions:

- "If this history book is supposed to be about the whole world, then how come so much of it is about only a little part of it?"
- "What if some of the people on the jury just go along with the other people on the jury even though they think the Los Angeles Police Department is innocent?"

They also surfaced when students delved into their projects:

- "Can we bring in things from home to add to our Mohen-jo-daro artifacts?"
- "We want the whole class to be in our last skit."

These are the moments of my student teaching term that flash back to me. And in the questions that students began to ask—why the history books were the way they were, why the principal could set a "no shorts allowed" rule when the building was steaming, why they could clean up the garbage only on the playground and not in the park across the street without parental permission—were the very definitions and enactment of empowerment.

While I struggled through technical issues of grading, management, and scheduling during my student teaching term, I also struggled to "create space" to teach a non-stereotypical perspective of Islam, Mohen-jo-daro, Rodney King, Columbus, Earth, and Native American issues, while teaching the required material. The latter struggle most stands out in my teaching journal and in my mind. But as I was working through this process of learning how to teach, "what worked and what didn't," I also began to understand the overall structure of the school and how it, like the mandated, objectified, and deskilled curriculum, limits teachers in important ways.

THE HIERARCHY

During my three months at South, the teachers and administrators were beginning a process of "reform." I was interested in finding out what this meant at South and in taking part in the early-morning discussions and meetings about "the reform" since issues of collaboration and school change would be an important part of my role as a teacher—if not at South then at the school/schools in which I would teach in the future. However, after Cindy and I went to the first morning meeting together, the principal, Mr. Elson, suggested privately to Cindy that student teachers should not attend the next meetings since our presence might interfere with the reform process or discourage other teachers from speaking openly.

Mr. Elson's suggestion disturbed me at the time because, as already indicated, I was eager to know how the issue of reform would be addressed and enacted at South. To this day, I am not sure why it was so important that student teachers not attend the reform meetings. Perhaps there was a valid reason. At the time, both I and my advisor from UEP were simply disturbed and discouraged. However, as I spent more time at South and began to get a sense of the overall power structure of the school, the reform meeting incident became less surprising.

An overall feeling of collaboration and unity among teachers and between teachers and administrators did not exist in the everyday routine of South Elementary. There were some teachers who were friends and who worked together on a few projects or field trips (such as when Cindy, another teacher, and I decided to work on the Earth theme), and one of the program coordinators often provided supplemental resources for the gifted classes. For the most part, however, teachers worked in the isolation of their own classrooms. Only during teacher evaluation periods did Mr. Elson regularly enter the classroom. Only on the playground, in the lunchroom, and during school assemblies did students regularly meet students from other classrooms.

Cindy and I talked on several occasions about how Mr. Elson's stern, businesslike, and aloof manner was, outwardly at least, cold and threatening. We talked about the ways in which enthusiastic, involved principals could facilitate an entirely different, more creative and collaborative tone in schools. Despite these conversations about the need to create an open atmosphere for teaching/learning, Cindy was constantly aware of and concerned about Mr. Elson's view of her teaching and her class. For instance, after the school assembly in which our class performed pieces of poetry written by African-Americans, Cindy was disturbed that Mr. Elson did not comment on her class's performance as he did to other teachers after their performances. She knew that what the class had done was exceptional and educational, yet the fact that Mr. Elson hadn't complimented their work seemed, for Cindy, to change the overall success of the performance.

Seeking encouragement and appreciating compliments from our colleagues is undoubtedly important and affects our motivation. And indeed many other teachers and students commented on the success of the class's performance. But it was important for Cindy to receive a sign of approval from Mr. Elson. In other cases, when Cindy was enthusiastic about students' interests in a particular project or activity we were working on, such as during the Mohen-jo-daro archeology conference, Cindy would often ask the principal or an administrator to come into the classroom and see what we were doing. Instead of being part of a "join our project" kind of invitation, the presence of Mr. Elson during our activities usually became more of a performance in which Cindy, the students, and I were cautious about what we said and did, careful to impress first. His presence would take away from the aims of our activities.

This pressure to please the principal, who was otherwise disconnected from the activities in our classroom, revealed the hierarchy and the power structure of the teacher/principal/administrator relationship. The students in my class were keenly aware of the power relationship between Cindy and Mr. Elson. Because the class cared about Cindy, they too were always on the lookout, being especially careful that when Mr. Elson was around, Cindy looked like a teacher who always had her class under control.

One particular instance that comes to mind is the time we were working on group art projects using yarn and starch. Because of the collaborative nature of the project, students were making more noise than if they had been working independently. And because of the sticky nature of starch, students were constantly leaving the classroom to wash their hands. At some point, Scottie spotted Mr. Elson in the hallway. He came back into the room and quickly, nervously, and privately told Cindy and me, "He's coming! I saw Mr. Elson in the hallway." Then he told his classmates, "Everyone be quiet or Ms. Tenner and Ms. Shah will get in trouble!" This comment and Scottie's genuine concern illustrates the real tensions that existed between teachers and administrators at South—teachers and administrators who are, theoretically, working together toward a common goal of educating and learning.

The practice of administrators' "checking on" teachers was present not only in the evaluation procedures and the monthly tests but also in the policy that required teachers to turn in their lesson plan books to Mr. Elson at the beginning of each week. Mr. Elson would check the teachers' plans and "okay" them with red ink. Teachers were then to pick up their books from the office. This policy reinforced South's understanding of teachers as subordinates, the hierarchical structure in which administrators govern teachers and teachers govern students.

Rather than living in a relationship of collaboration, the feeling that we are all in this school to prepare students to create and live democratically and responsibly, many teachers were constantly working to get the attention, compliments, and approval of the principal and administrators in the same way that students in traditional classrooms vie to become the "teacher's favorite"—both situations are about passivity and control and neither situation is about empowerment and action.

As I became more aware of this hierarchy, I began asking questions about the structure of South and of schools in general: If Mr. Elson is otherwise not involved with the process, actions, and directions of our classroom, why should he be the ultimate observer/judge of our work as a class? Do the hierarchical models of business management, government bureaucracy, and militaristic structure mesh with the aim of public schools to educate and empower democratic citizens? What are the alternatives that have been attempted? Which alternatives work?"

While I continued to think about these issues, I started brainstorming with my UEP advisor about what policies, events, and changes would make this power situation more equitable and more conducive to a teaching/learning community. In many other city schools the administrators, principals, teachers, and students interact more frequently and in more collaborative ways. Perhaps the "reform" talk at South would move toward this kind of atmosphere. But in the meantime I started thinking: If I were to stay at South or begin working at a school with a similar power structure, what could I do to move toward creating dialogue, debate, and community not only in my classroom but in my school and community?

HOPE AND CHANGE: COLLECTIVE EFFORTS

The early morning reform discussions could potentially work toward more open communication between teachers and teachers, as well as teachers and administrators, and toward an atmosphere celebrating the collective. While I was not involved in these discussions, I did think about other changes/additions that could make South feel like more of a community of collaboration.

One of the main deficiencies or obstacles to creating teacher dialogue at South was the lack of a common lounge or a room where teachers could come together to get to know each other informally, perhaps to share teaching resources or read current articles in educational journals and newspapers. Since teachers were required to sit with their classes during the lunch period, the lunchroom cafeteria did not provide this type of space— teachers simply bought their lunches in the teacher cafeteria and took their seats in the student cafeteria. Teachers at South had at least one "prep period" per day while their class was at library, gym, and so forth. Instead of isolated work in their own classrooms during this prep period, teachers might work together in the teachers' lounge. Although this seems a relatively simple reform, and although many schools do have teachers' lounges, the lack of a space for teachers to come together at South reinforced the non-collaborative aspects of the school culture discussed earlier. In this space, teachers may begin to move toward sharing ideas, responsibilities, visions of change, moments of controversy, and plans of action.

In addition to this space within the school, teachers need to create communal space outside the school. Involvement in teachers' unions and Local School Councils is central to connecting with other teachers, and other people invested in the education of students. However, creating space for teachers outside the school also means developing several Teacher Centers, perhaps funded collaboratively with local universities committed to collaboration. These centers could provide alternative educational texts, materials, equipment, and seminars for teachers in a particular area.

If the realities of some current city school budgets do not allow for photocopying, updated texts, and other necessary resources, and if we are truly concerned about educating students in equitable ways, then Teacher Centers may provide a realistic option. In addition to providing equipment for teacher use, similar to the movement toward collaboration in teachers' lounges, Teacher Centers could expand this model of dialogue among teachers beyond the school.

Also, there are resources available from several organizations and institutions such as the World Without War Council, University of Wisconsin African Studies Program, National Precollegiate Japan Project Network, Cornell College Latin American Studies Program, ACCESS, University of Chicago Center for Middle East Studies, and so on, available to teachers who want to educate students more equitably than standard school curricula allow. Many teachers do not have access to such organizations, alternative resources, and innovative ideas. Serving as a connection between teachers and educational organizations and projects, Teacher Centers would be invaluable, opening possibilities of collaboration between various schools and federal and local organizations.

Additionally, while I was doing my student teaching, my UEP advisor recommended that I visit several elementary and high schools and observe other classrooms in the city. The experience of seeing other teaching styles and school organization models made me aware of the range of possibilities from traditional, teacher-centered classrooms to less structured alternative schools. Instead of just observing this range of teaching/learning, I was inevitably drawn into the process of thinking about where my teaching styles fall on the range that I observed, how I might want to change my methods and structures, and so forth. In other words, observing other classroom realities pulled me from a micro-perspective of my experiences at South to a macro-perspective of school structure, and teaching and learning, in various schools in Chicago. This broader perspective gave more meaning, context, and possibility to my own teaching.

At the Teacher Centers, exposure to teachers from other schools with some similar and some different school realities would also facilitate getting a fuller perspective on schools and teaching. Teacher Centers could also be a place for parents, teachers, administrators, community members, and students to intersect in conversations and planning about schools' structure and curricula. If we do not see or hear of schools that work differently than ours, it is more difficult to envision changes in the structure and workings of our own schools.

REFLECTING AND MOVING

I often look back through the words in my teaching journal, the margin notes in books I read in education courses, or the quotations I recorded or highlighted—words of Paulo Freire, Sylvia Ashton-Warner, Maxine Greene, John Dewey, and fellow educational studies students at Knox, words that outline a different kind of school, a different kind of world. When I re-read and re-hear these words and compare these visions of teaching and social change to my student teaching experience and now to my teaching career, I consistently ask myself if I did/am doing enough. That is, while I was studying teaching/learning/schooling in college and through books, these words were moving and directing; they embodied what I wanted my role as a teacher to be about. But did I, do I, and will I, when it is time to connect action to these words, significantly move toward a different social vision of community, equality, and justice? Am I being "idealistic" and naive about how I will teach?

Teaching full-time has indeed provided important insights and revised some of my perspectives on what liberating classrooms look like. For instance, as an undergraduate I was extremely critical of teachers' exercising power in the classroom. During observations in schools, I filled my journal with critical notes about the strict adherence to the rule of raising your hand and waiting for the teacher to call on you before you speak and the militaristic demand for straight lines with boys on one side and girls on the other. These procedures demonstrated an undemocratic lack of autonomy for students and teachers. When I am a teacher, I wrote, these rules will not be a part of my classroom. Students will learn on their own how to wait until their turn to speak, how to engage in effective dialogue, how to exit the room and walk in halls in an appropriate way.

Now, as a fifth-grade teacher, I have learned that these ideas were naive and not rooted in an understanding of a 32-student, urban classroom reality. However, I have not abandoned the commitment to a more participatory and cooperative classroom that guided my thoughts as an undergraduate. Instead, I am learning that teaching students to take responsibility for their voices and actions is a process. Now, I also require students to stand in line outside my classroom. However, we line up by teams, not by sex. And students do have to raise their hands and wait to be called on before they speak. However, students call on each other in a manageable way. There is no denying that I still have power and the responsibility to monitor in both of these situations. For now, I have learned, there has to be a combination of introducing students to ideas of voice, participation, and responsibility, on the one hand, and relating to what they expect a teacher to be, being honest about my authority as a teacher, on the other. This again is about creating space—not between mandated objectives and worthwhile learning but between what students know and expect and the possibilities of a democratic and liberating classroom. As an undergraduate, I would have called this a copout, not radical enough.

Democratic, culturally relevant, and empowering schooling is radically different from the current realities in most public schools; we have a long way to go from here to there. However, these visions and possibilities of egalitarian educational systems and an egalitarian society do have a place in the everyday struggle to make schools democratic and empowering institutions—they are the commitments, goals, and images that guide the way we structure our classrooms and curriculum.

The process of changing public schools from the current factory model where students are controlled, processed, and told what to know and believe to models more conducive to democracy and discovery cannot be achieved without engaging teachers, students, administrators, and communities in a dialogue about what is and what should be. For instance, I am part of a group of teachers at my school working to revamp our report card process. We began to think about what we believe evaluation should be about and what our current evaluation procedures actually measure. We are hoping to move toward a more meaningful and portfolio-type assessment in which students, parents, and teachers participate. Until we begin to change current models of education and enter the type of dialogue that takes place in some communities and school councils, the theme of teachers' struggling to make better worlds in schools will be limited to "creating space" instead of creating widespread, immediate change.

As we create space beyond mandated objectives for worthwhile activities, space to share resources, space for our own empowerment and for student empowerment, space for students to exercise democracy and responsibility in classrooms and a world often diametrically opposed to these fundamental rights—as we create this space, perhaps as groups of teachers, as schools and communities, we can begin to collectively examine our perspectives, envision possibility, and move toward significant transformations in our worlds.

NOTES

1. These figures were obtained from the Chicago Public School Board, personal communication.

2. The fact that I was in a gifted classroom with the best texts, resources, and space to include innovative methods and ideas was also disturbing and overwhelming. If I was so discouraged by the texts being used in the gifted program, what were the neighborhood students facing each day?

REFERENCES

Ashton-Warner, S. (1963). *Teacher*. New York: Simon and Schuster.

Bigelow, B. (1991). Discovering Columbus: Re-reading the past. In B. Bigelow, B. Miner, & B. Peterson (Eds.), *Rethinking Columbus: Teaching about the 500th anniversary of Columbus's arrival in America* (pp. 6–9). Milwaukee: Rethinking Schools.

Dewey, J. (1902/1956). *The child and the curriculum*. Chicago: University of Chicago Press.

Explorations. (1986). *Reading workbook*. Boston: Houghton Mifflin.

Freire, P. (1990). *Education for critical consciousness*. New York: Continuum.

Freire, P. (1992). *Pedagogy of the oppressed*. New York: Continuum.

Lorde, A. (1977, December). *The transition of silence into language and action*. Paper presented at the Modern Language Association's "Lesbianism and Literature" Panel, Chicago.

Shah, U. (1991). Unpublished journal entries for Educational Studies 310, Knowledge and Power: Perspectives on Curriculum.

Thompson, J. (1992). Blacks only one group ignored in history class. *New Expressions, 16*(2), 5.

World Past to Present. (1989). Lexington, MA: D.C. Heath Co.

FOUR

The Rock House:
Barriers in Education and
Their Demolition

Joni Garlock

I moved from Ohio to Illinois five years ago, and since that time I have been able to visit my father only about twice a year. We do, however, speak once a week by phone. These conversations have become more and more important to me as I get older. I realize how much my dad has learned and seen in his 50-odd years, and have grown to respect him very much. I remember in high school I didn't think he knew anything. He went to work as a tile setter every day and came home every night. I didn't think we had anything in common. Now when we speak we share stories about our jobs, our experiences, and our feelings.

Several weeks before school started my dad told me about an interesting house he was working on. It seemed the builder wanted to cover the outside of the house with large white rocks. Because each rock weighed approximately 100 pounds, it had to be individually set in place and supported until the mortar hardened. My dad reported that nothing would be able to penetrate this wall once it was completed.

Once my school year started, in the fall of 1992, I forgot about the rock-covered house and became caught up with school and the adventure of being a first-year teacher. It wasn't until Christmas break that I thought about that house again. As I was trying to decide what to focus on for this chapter, the rock-house kept creeping into my thoughts. I sensed a connection between it and teaching.

The house was impermeable to any outside force, the rocks forming a barrier between the inhabitants within and the world outside. Teaching, and the entire educational system, create barriers of their own. There are the barriers built up among teachers, students and teachers, teachers and the administration, and teachers and parents. Instead of keeping out intruders as the rock-house does, the barriers that occur in education keep out knowledge and creative thinking. And just as the house was built rock by rock, the educational barriers are slowly and, in many cases, deliberately put into place.

ROCK NUMBER 1: THE EGG-CARTON BARRIER

The rock-house was built using separate stones, which together formed its entire facade. Similarly, in schools teachers have separate areas called classrooms that, collectively, make up the school building. When teachers begin to use their classrooms as barriers against the rest of their school, the egg-carton syndrome has taken over. Some teachers believe that once they enter their room they are safe from outside influences and disruptions. On many occasions, this concept is carried outside of the room to the point that a teacher may refuse to accept any outside stimulus without even considering its benefits or disadvantages. Usually these teachers have been working for several years and have strengthened their barrier (just as mortar strengthens the rock wall) to such an extent that no amount of pushing can break through.

I came across several teachers in this category during my first year of teaching. One in particular comes to mind, whom I will call Mr. Burns. I was in the teachers' lounge (another barrier, discussed below) explaining an upcoming art show and the particulars surrounding the event. Several teachers were interested in my comments because students from my school had never participated in a show before. Before I could finish my description, Mr. Burns burst into the conversation and asked, "Is this 'show' taking place on a school day?" When I said it was, Mr. Burns immediately began a lengthy and offensive diatribe about "extracurricular activities" and how they should not occur during school hours. I explained that this was not an extracurricular activity and the students would benefit from seeing other artists' work. I tried to make him see that experience, in many cases, is a better teacher than a book or a filmstrip. I explained that art, or any other subject, should not be segregated from other disciplines. Art encompasses history, sociology, anthropology, and many other areas.

I continued my conversation with Mr. Burns by describing a project that the high school students were working on and how worthwhile it was, although most of the work was taking place outside the classroom. In this case, we were first approached by the principal of the junior high who wanted a mural painted on the wall between the science rooms. We began by thinking of five topics that would be interesting to junior high students and that would fit in to the atmosphere of the school. We chose the environment, fantasy, a painting of the town, a painting of the school, and famous people from Illinois. We then made up ballots with all five ideas and asked the junior high students to vote for their favorite. We felt that this would be the best way to include the junior high students in the project. We did not want them to feel that the mural had been purely a high school project.

When the ballots were counted, the environment came out as the winner. We began to research animals, plants, and environmental issues that we felt would fit into our design. We later decided to focus on endangered species to enhance the importance of the project. I was extremely impressed with the level of enthusiasm expressed by the students. They brought in so much information that soon my desk was piled with books, posters, and pamphlets. At that point we felt we had enough information and so began to sketch out our ideas on paper.

At this point in my story I stopped to point out to Mr. Burns that we began sketching only after we had done many tasks that most people would not think of as "art-related." We conducted research in biology, politics, environmentalism, botany, and many other areas. Most of our work had taken place outside the classroom. It was only after two weeks of preparation that we began sketching and other "art-related" procedures. Because we had delved into the sciences and history, our project was much more convincing and accurate. I wanted him to understand that this approach to teaching encourages interest in areas beyond the original discipline. It helped students to understand the social, political, and moral beliefs of their society and how they can change or accept them. I went on to say that it may not be important that Johnny knows how to do his algebra equations perfectly if he cannot integrate all that he has learned into a cohesive whole. Life is not set up in a series of unrelated incidents; it is a free-flowing stream of interrelated situations. Why, then, should we teach students in a fractured, incongruous style?

After I finished describing my experience, Mr. Burns explained the reasons behind his teaching style. He told me that he had come from the "old school" where it is believed that the 3-Rs are the most important thing educators must pass on to their students. He went on to say that the basics must be stressed in education and that "extras" like art and music are of lesser importance. It was obvious to me that Mr. Burns had built up his egg-carton barrier to a point that no one (especially an art teacher) could break through. Just as the rocks kept intruders from entering the house, Mr. Burns kept students from becoming integrated learners.

These types of barriers take time to build. Teachers, for the most part, do not start their teaching careers this way. Most new teachers have a wide spectrum of strategies to use in their quest to teach their specific area of concentration. If they decide to break out of their egg-cartons and encompass multiple areas of learning they may become better teachers. If they do not they will be limiting their students and themselves. Avoiding this trap is difficult. It is easy to blame it on time constraints, lack of money, or the students. However, it boils down to the teacher's commitment as an educator. What can the teacher do to make the lessons interesting? How can the teacher avoid the barrier of static, uninteresting lessons? Who can blame a student for being bored with a lesson if the teacher is bored with it because he or she has taught the same thing for 10 years? The material is not what is boring; it is the method of presentation that is uninteresting.

There are several things that can be done to help a new teacher avoid this barrier. For example, keeping a journal of curricular experiences can assist the teacher in remembering what lessons were attempted and how they were implemented. However, writing down what you did and how the students reacted is only part of what should be recorded. Teachers also need to reflect on what else was going on at that time: Was it prom week? Was it the first sunny day after a week of rain? Was my attitude at the time of the lesson influential? It helps to ask students what they thought of the activity. They may have suggestions for how to make it better. Sometimes an idea that may not have worked would work better at a different place in the curriculum.

Another idea to avoid the egg-carton barrier is to seek advice from other teachers. Fortunately, all teachers are not committed to the isolation of subjects and people. Some may even want to participate in a joint project. Since many teachers are setting up their curriculum based around themes or topics, it makes sense that all disciplines should be included. For example, a teacher may base a week of teaching on the topic of water. All lessons relate to the topic but encompass many areas or fields. The first day may concern the interaction between water and plant life. The second may include animals, and so on. This type of curriculum is ideal in terms of including other teachers and their areas of expertise. In my own case, it was clear that the mural project was interesting to other teachers as well as students. Many teachers offered resources from their own subject area expertise. For example, the science teacher helped us check the accuracy of the plants and animals that we drew.

I have found that teaching broad concepts rather than limiting lessons to art or math or science takes place more often in elementary and middle school than it does at the high school level. Elementary teachers usually have the same students all day and teach virtually all subjects. Once the students enter high school they rotate from teacher to teacher, each of whom teaches individual subjects with little, if any, common ground.

Although the mural was an "outside" project, I try to encompass all areas of learning in my art classes. We read about the history of a certain period of art. We discuss the people, their culture, and why they chose to create certain art forms. We decide how we can interpret what happened then and make it meaningful now. And we express what we learned in a project that relates to our investigation. Sometimes the projects are meaningful to us, sometimes we realize they are not working. Quite often, as we progress through our inquiry, I feel that we are spiraling into nowhere. At times it is very difficult for me not to retreat into my safe egg-carton and lecture on Monet and his water lilies. I have a feeling that my students would look at me like I was crazy if I went into this stereotypical teacher mode. They usually have that reaction on those occasions when I "lose it" and tell everyone to sit down and be quiet.

Although it may at first be difficult to break the egg-carton barrier, in the long run it makes teaching and learning more interesting and worthwhile. Rather than lecturing to a sea of bored faces, the teacher can interact with students and learn along with them. For example, during an exploration of Egyptian art, two students in my classroom created a video of an "actual" archaeological dig. They knew a pilot who flew them to "Egypt" where they uncovered "artifacts" dating back to Egyptian times. The video was extremely creative and showed not only what the students learned about Egyptian art but their knowledge of video, aviation, editing, and acting. The rest of the class and I were not only entertained but learned about things to which we would otherwise not have been exposed. I was amazed that my students had taken my model of teaching and used it in their own project. They had explored many areas that were not "art-related" and come up with an informative and interesting video.

ROCK NUMBER 2: STUDENTS VS. THE SYSTEM

The egg-carton barrier is, in my view, the most disruptive influence on students' education. However, there are other barriers that may be more subtle but are also harmful to students' educational growth. On my first day as a new teacher I was barraged by stories about the previous art teacher. I was told that her students would climb the walls, steal her keys, leave her class—never to return, and ask for, and receive, passes to the Dairy Queen. Teachers would nudge me and say, "You know you will get all the bad ones dumped on you." I was also told that almost all the special education students would be in my classes. Needless to say, I was very scared—and very curious. My first-hour class was calm and mild. It consisted of the usual "good kids" who had adapted to the school system and thrived within it. My second class was slightly more aggressive. It contained several students who had been labeled behavior problems and two who had recently been released from prison. These students were floundering and trying to find a place in the system. My third class was even more active. It consisted of students who either had smokers' breath or wore "Megadeath" T-shirts. These students had seen what the system had to offer and rejected it.

After the first week or so I began to wonder how we were going to accomplish anything this year. With all the different personalities, what would happen? I had two advantages that not all teachers have. First, I was a new teacher with no prior knowledge of the students (except for the horror stories told in the teachers' lounge). Second, I was somewhat of a rebel in high school and could relate to the way students resented or rejected the system. With these two things in mind, I began the year trying to break through some of the barriers the system created. I believed that once the students saw that I did not blindly accept all rules handed out, they would begin to trust me and learn to find their own niche. Also, once they saw that I would not judge them according to what they had done in the past maybe they would begin to break out from their mold of "trouble maker" or "goodie-goodie."

As I look back on my first year, one student comes to mind over and over again. "Sam" came to my class the first day and informed me that he and the previous art teacher had not gotten along. At one point he became so angry with this teacher that he threw a desk in her direction and was subsequently suspended. I told Sam that the tables we were now using in the art room were fairly heavy and that he might injure himself trying to pick one of them up. I think he was shocked that I didn't answer by listing the rules of the room and telling him anyone breaking those rules would be removed.

Throughout the first quarter we discussed the different rules of the school, both written and unwritten, and questioned their fairness. By breaking the code of silent acceptance some teachers like to maintain, we began to form a friendship. We eventually started whole-class discussions that became a way for students to speak out. They began to see that their opinions mattered. One discussion focused on the idea of developing an Art III class for the following year. The students pursued the idea by sending out petitions and talking to the administration, eventually getting approval for the class. We found that when we recognized and discussed the barriers in the school, they began to break down. Further, when something positive came from the discussions, a truly valuable learning experience took place. These discussions also helped us become acquainted with each other's ideas, hopes, and dreams and, in the case of Sam, we became friends. I do not think a teacher has to be a friend to all of his or her students, however; indeed, with so many different personalities in one room, that seems impossible. I do believe that all students should be treated with respect. Sometimes this is difficult, especially if students inform you that if you make them angry they will become violent. By breaking through the normal barriers of a school or a classroom, teachers can begin to show students that there are other ways to look at things and different ways to react to a situation.

During many of my education classes we discussed how we would implement our ideas into the seemingly rigid structure known as "the school system," without losing our position. I remember feeling very frustrated because there was not a definite answer for how to accomplish this. I thought that whatever had to be done would have to be earth-shattering. I realize now that less is sometimes more. The examples above may appear small but were they, and others like them, carried from one individual classroom throughout the school, and beyond, they would not be insignificant.

ROCK NUMBER 3: TEACHERS VS. THE SYSTEM

When I first began thinking about the barriers facing teachers, I felt that I personally had not experienced them. On closer investigation I realize that there are many levels to the barriers that exist in schools and that in certain ways I too was limited by the school system. One level encompasses the classroom itself—the everyday goings on. On this level I thought we were fairly free to explore material as we wanted to. We could choose what to study, when to study it, and how to study. Another level includes how and by whom the curriculum is chosen. At this level we begin to lose some of our freedom. The final level concerns the basic procedures that every school has to utilize to maintain some form of "control." At this level we lose almost all of our freedom. This includes the need to administer hall passes, bathroom passes, discipline codes, dress codes, and so on.

These three levels taken together make up the school system and can create a barrier for teachers. It is the task of the teacher and the students to infiltrate the system so that creative, meaningful learning can take place. If a visitor were to walk into my classroom on any given day he or she might see total chaos: paint everywhere, students standing, sitting, talking, thinking. We have been able to choose our way of learning without a great deal of outside input from the administration. This is not the case in all schools, however. I feel very lucky to have a "hands-off" principal. There are periods when I do not even see him for three or four days at a time. When I first started teaching I wondered why the administration would trust me to teach 80 or so students. Although it was frightening at first, the freedom that we have has been beneficial to our learning process.

So there I was, believing that I had side-stepped the barriers mentioned above. My classes were learning and I was feeling that this was the best teaching job ever. Then came the fateful day when I was called to a meeting to discuss the new STATE GOALS FOR TEACHING THE FINE ARTS. At the meeting I was told that new goals, along with some method of evaluating them, were to be written by the Art Department. Grades 4, 8, and 10 were to be evaluated. Well, since *I am* the Art Department, the task lay on my shoulders. So much for freedom in the classroom. The arts were to be tainted by STANDARDIZED TESTS. The system had begun to place barriers in front of my students and me that would hinder our learning experiences.

As I progressed through the processes of developing goals, having them reviewed, rewriting, and finally developing an evaluation, I became more and more agitated. I began to question the value of standardized tests in any discipline. They put limits on the students by questioning only one, limited kind of knowing—the memorization of facts. Rather than testing this small part of learning, perhaps students should be evaluated in a way that takes into consideration *all* the accomplishments of an entire quarter or semester. Rather than focusing on a few isolated facts, why not look at their growth as persons and students? For example, on occasion a student will express a feeling of inadequacy during a project. I try to explain that as long as he or she is trying to do his or her best, nothing else matters. When I am forced to grade I always expound on the positive things of the work along with suggestions about how the student can improve on what he or she is trying to express. However, if students are forced to prove themselves on a standardized test, this philosophy doesn't mean much. In fact, it amounts to just another contradiction that the students are fed everyday by the school system.

As I thought about this dilemma, I decided to share my feelings with my students and find out their perspectives. I explained that I did not believe in testing, and why, and they agreed. They felt, as I did, that the things that were most important could not be tested in this way. I felt they were the seasoned veterans who were teaching me the ropes. After our discussion we all felt better and agreed to take the test with a grain of salt.

This experience taught me a great deal and helped to break down a few barriers between my students and me. I really believe that one of the most important aspects of teaching is realizing that you do not know everything. Allow your students to teach you, let them help you become a better teacher and a better human being.

The final aspect of the teacher-versus-the-system barrier concerns the basic way a school is run. It is at this level that philosophical analysis and creativity are reduced to a stack of hall passes and the sound of a bell. Unfortunately, this is also the hardest barrier to get around. You cannot tell your principal that you wish to have two-hour classes instead of 50-minute ones. You also cannot bring in a nude model for your students to draw from. Granted, not all schools are on an 8-period, 180-day schedule, but those that are may need to reevaluate their formats. There have been many attempts at doing this—Montessori, open classrooms, interdisciplinary courses, and so forth. It is beyond the scope of this chapter to delve into these alternatives. The point, however, is simple. Can students learn effectively—especially at the fragmented level of the high school where classes are divided into disciplines—that everything is related? Will students learn if they are afraid to voice their opinions because the teacher may not agree or because "We don't have time to talk about that right now, we have a test tomorrow"? Of course they will. They will learn that science and art and English have nothing to do with life, nor with each other. They will learn to avoid sharing their feelings, dreams, and emotions because it may be dangerous. It is up to classroom teachers to explain to their students the hidden curriculum at work in their schools. They know it exists, but if you problematize it with them, and let them know that you disagree with some of its messages, you can begin to develop a trust that goes beyond the scope of your subject matter.

ROCK NUMBER 4: TEACHERS VS. PARENTS

During my second semester of teaching I became immersed in a sexual abuse case involving one of my students. "Jill" and I had become close during the year and I was the person she chose to tell when the experience she was going through became too much for her to deal with. Together, we went through the process of notifying counselors and finally the Department of Children's Services. In the end the abuser basically had his hands slapped and was told not to go near the student's house.

At the beginning of the ordeal, when Jill was trying to tell me what was going on, I asked whether her parents knew. She said that she had told her mother, who did not believe her. When she had tried to tell her father he threw her up against the wall and told her to quit lying. She was afraid to go to the school counselors because she knew they would contact her parents. The only family support that she had was from a sickly grandmother. Jill was afraid to tell her grandmother because she did not know if the grandmother could physically take the shock.

I had heard about cases such as this, but they somehow did not seem real. Now that I was personally involved it was hard not to become physically ill from the thought of the act of abuse itself, as well as the lack of support on the part of Jill's parents. I felt frightened every night when I left school knowing that she would be going home to the same environment. This experience taught me a lot about the relationship between students and their parents. Although this example does not precisely embody a teachers-versus-parents barrier, it offers insight into some parents' attitudes toward the school system. The student involved in this case had parents who did not trust the school system or other social service agencies, like Children's Services. They chose to handle the situation their own way—essentially by ignoring it. Meanwhile, Jill continued to suffer. Parents often feel alienated from schools, which causes them to react in one of several ways. They may react as the parents mentioned above by choosing to handle a problem their own way; they may decide to fight the system through legal means or through the school board; they may decide to wash their hands of a situation and let the school handle the problem; or they may decide to send their child to a private school. Some parents do choose to work with members of the school system when trying to solve a problem involving their child, but a significant number feel the school is a place where they are not welcome.

My experience with Jill and her parents made me realize several things. Although children are in school most of the day, they do have to go home. For many children home is not a very supportive place to be. If only, through education, we could teach parents that the time children spend outside of school is at least as important as the time spent in school, both parents and their children would benefit. We need to develop a network that extends beyond the school and involves everyone in the community.

The educational system should not be looked at as an island where only certain people are welcome. We need to find a way to break the barrier that keeps parents away from school. I know several teachers who would prefer never to talk to a parent. I can understand this attitude if one is faced with an irate mother or father, but we must look at what made that mother so angry, what alienated that father in the first place. Many parents feel the same barriers that the students feel during the school day. Usually when parents do show up at school it is because their child has been accused of some infraction. They should come to school for positive reasons, not just negative ones. I have found that calling the parents of so-called troublemakers to tell them something positive about their child usually results in surprised but pleased parents. I have also sent invitations to parents to come into my classroom and to our annual art show. Although only a few came, they were parents who usually do not come to school-related events at all.

I know that there are many parents who feel that what goes on in school is not their concern. For those parents it may be impossible to break the barrier between themselves and the school. Unfortunately, their behavior is usually reflected in their children and the cycle continues when they have children of their own. But if teachers can reach some parents who would otherwise have remained aloof, they have accomplished something beneficial for both student and parents.

THE WALL COMES DOWN

This chapter is dedicated to the exploration of the barriers that exist in education. It is also a testament to the everyday struggles of a new teacher. Although the barriers are many, I believe many teachers have the tools necessary to break through. We have to be human beings with our students and let them see that we are learning alongside them. We also have to show them that mistakes are a large part of learning and that we understand and accept their mistakes as part of this process. Schools must change into something other than a compartmentalized box of non-related spaces. When we integrate all areas of learning, students can understand relationships in our world at a much deeper level. Schools also must become places where parents and other members of the community can come to share knowledge, concerns, and suggestions. These ideas, and the others mentioned in this chapter, are ways that I have found to improve the education and lives of my students. I hope that when I look back after 15 years of teaching many of the barriers will have broken down. I keep thinking about the rock-house my father told me about and I hope that the barriers I have discussed are not as sturdy as his wall of rocks. I do believe that teachers can make a difference. I know this is a worn-out cliché, but we must believe it to be true or there may not be any hope. As the rocks of education are cemented into place we, as teachers, must be the sledgehammers that break through. Some of us may swing harder than others but the fact that we're swinging at all is what makes a difference.

FIVE

Building Bridges Toward Democracy

Noelle Hawk Jaddaoui

Teaching is an occupation for the curious. A person has to have a healthy curiosity to be good at it, to search and research for the best principles and approaches to teaching. Such searching/researching distinguishes teaching from many other occupations.

As students of educational studies at Knox College in the late 1980s, my classmates and I studied the history and philosophy of education in the United States. We studied the development of compulsory education and we explored the expectations that our society has had of its schools. We asked ourselves, "What is the purpose of education?" and "What can schools do to accomplish that purpose?"

It would be unrealistic to suggest that there exists only one purpose for education, for that would deny the struggle that has always existed concerning what schools should teach and how teaching should be undertaken. Yet, throughout my coursework, one central theme kept reappearing among our readings and discussions. That theme concerned the social and educational meanings of democracy. It spoke to me; I came to believe that the best and most important life work in which I could engage was teaching, helping shape our nation's youth into active citizens to form a peaceful, democratic world.

Ask 10 people to define "democracy" and it's likely you will get 10 different answers. To some, democracy means being free from external constraints. Others believe democracy means being able to make choices, such as where to live or what kind of job to have. Still others equate democracy with the right to vote.

Dictionaries, a source we are usually trained to depend on for determining important meanings, differ little one from another. The *Webster's*

Intermediate Dictionary (1977) defines democracy as "1a: government by the people; esp: rule of the majority b: government in which the supreme power is vested in the people and exercised by them directly or indirectly through representation" (p. 195).

Most Americans accept these definitions without serious question. We have been taught since we were young to make group decisions by voting, counting hands or ballots, and doing whatever the majority wants to do. As adults we continue casting our ballots, electing representatives to run our government in our absence, expecting that they will listen to our concerns and conduct themselves loyally on our behalf. We've never seriously considered participating directly in self-government, except those few who have run for an elected office.

However, becoming an elected official is difficult. These days it seems to require the right "connections" coupled with an image-management campaign requiring massive fund-raising efforts. The average American starts the process at a disadvantage even before his or her political position on issues is presented. Self-government and, therefore, democracy as a way of life have become seriously jeopardized by current practices.

I want to help us move away from the notion of a representative form of political life in which citizens rely on the decisions made by a few elite, expert, elected individuals, assuming that they are all-knowing and have our best interests at heart. I want to think of democracy in a participatory sense, in which all citizens take part, actively, in discussions and actions concerning issues and events that inevitably affect their lives (Barber, 1984). My vision of democracy also encourages individuals to work together toward a "common good" rather than individually toward private interests and personal gain (Bellah, Madsen, Sullivan, Swidler, & Tipton, 1985). Environmental deterioration, a ballooning national debt, increasing violent crime, and continued homelessness are symptoms of neglect of that common good.

We desperately need citizens who can generate ideas that can lead us toward alternative ways of life that will save our lives and the lives of the generations who will follow us. We need people who can think, feel, imagine, and create. We need people who care, who feel connected to the world in which they live, who believe they have the power to enact the changes they will want to make. As a teacher I have a unique opportunity to create the kind of environment in which young people can grow and become the kind of active citizens that we need.

About to enter my sixth year of teaching, I have begun to understand what I have done and need to do to develop a practice consistent with my theoretical outlook. What has taken me so long? Contrary to popular belief, memorizing a finite set of facts or procedures and passing an exam do not make someone an effective teacher. Rather, it is an ongoing process of practice, reflection, and constant reevaluation based on knowledge of current research, philosophical beliefs, and reconsideration of practice.

In reflecting on the past four years of my career, I realize that I have been very busy in search of ways to become a more democratic educator. I started, during my grueling first year of teaching, by building bridges. As a resource teacher of English as a Second Language (ESL) for children in grades 1 to 5, I was very isolated. The process of building these bridges was crucial to my survival as a teacher and it taught me introductory lessons about how to make participatory democracy come to life.

The first bridge I had to build went back to my college classroom perspective. I was trying to connect it with the one I had begun developing during my first year of full-time, full-responsibility public school teaching. There were many things related to becoming a school community member that college readings and classroom discussions couldn't convey. In retrospect, I know there is no way that teacher education programs, even one as progressive as mine, can fully prepare people for all that will happen during that first year.

During one of our final courses at Knox College, Professor Beyer tried to address this problem. He asked us, "So, at this point, do any of you have any questions . . . concerns . . . fears [about teaching]?" He punctuated his question with a coy laugh that, alone, told us "you haven't seen nothin' yet" and we had better take advantage of this rare opportunity to ask any questions we had. For several of us, student teaching was just around the corner, but even that experience often pales in comparison with the first year of the real thing!

None of us really knew what to ask. In answer to our silence, he said, "I don't know what I can tell you about what you can expect next." Again, that coy laugh, which I think was supposed to lighten the tone in the classroom, followed by the remarks, "I can only say it will be one of the hardest damn experiences you'll ever have. I really can't find the words to express it." We knew he wasn't intentionally trying to scare us. He was trying to prepare us for an inexplicably difficult experience. He was right on target! This bridge between my college days and my current practice is invaluable. I cross over and back daily, remembering what I've learned as I search for practices consistent with my educational outlook.

The next bridge I constructed was between my isolated ESL classroom and the classrooms housing the "regular" or "mainstream" teachers. Day after day I stared at my empty lesson plan book while it taunted and teased me. There's nothing worse than a blank page (which I went to college to learn how to fill) telling me how incompetent I am. I struggled to silence those empty pages one day at a time. Each day I tried new things. I was unsure of myself but eventually I crossed the bridge I'd built to the veterans' classrooms. I came away loaded with ideas to try. Some were invaluable, but many squarely contradicted my underdeveloped vision of a democratic, holistic classroom.

I did not build one bridge at a time. There was no time for it. As I was building the first two bridges, I was constructing many more, almost simultaneously. I built one between myself and my principal. He was my evaluator, which made this bridge important, but that quickly became a secondary reason for establishing it. Gaining and maintaining his support of the ESL program was far more essential. With his support I had the confidence to negotiate the difficulties of scheduling. Since I took children out of their regular classrooms for certain periods of time each day, it required a certain amount of flexibility—which was sometimes lacking—on the part of those teachers. Also, on occasion I found the need to discuss with teachers what was or was not reasonable to expect these Limited English Proficient students to do in their homerooms. My principal was someone from whom I could receive advice and support on such matters before interacting with my colleagues.[1]

I built another bridge between myself and the school secretary, who, as many in education acknowledge, is one of the crucial persons with whom to establish a relationship. She's the one who knows under what heading all the necessary forms are filed. She has, in her head, vital procedural information and names of various important contact people. She's also the keeper of "the key" to the supply closet, where construction paper, glue, scissors, tape, paper clips, writing paper, and so on, could be found. I could hardly function without her.

The bridge between myself and my students' parents was also important to establish. Parents can provide valuable insights about their children that allow teachers to see possible underlying causes of troubling behavior. Parents can also point out strengths their children have on which the teacher can build. Parents can be a strong source of support.

A bridge to the janitors had to be constructed in order for me to gain the needed assistance in redesigning and maintaining the condition of my classroom cubicle. These two men removed a folding partition that dramatically changed the feeling of my teaching space: two square office spaces were transformed into one uninterrupted learning rectangle. They also helped me replace 12 student desks with two rectangular tables from another building, allowing me to create useful, open floor space—a vital resource in any classroom.

The Parent-Teacher Association bridge helped me, during that first frantic year, to produce a gala event called International Night, in which food and dramatic, artistic entertainment were enjoyed by all. They organized a schoolwide, multiethnic potluck dinner while I set up, with the help of the fine arts staff, a program performed by the school's chorus, the Foreign Language Club, and my ESL students.

The final bridge I will mention, although there were many others, was the bridge that connected me to my district's bilingual department. Although the meetings were conducted in English, I could not fully comprehend their content for the first six or seven months, because of the myriad unfamiliar terms, abbreviations, and general cultural codes with which I was unfamiliar. This was a vital bridge; not only did it provide me with the procedural information I needed to know in order to run my particular program, but the colleagues I came to know through the department were the ones to whom I could relate most meaningfully and who could assist me with the challenges I faced.

I haven't stopped building bridges. It is possibly the single most important activity I have engaged in as a new teacher. During the summer of 1993, I began building the Golden Gateway of bridges. At National-Louis University I became involved in the Chicago Area Writing Project through their Summer Institute. This institute was a series of graduate-level classes that, once completed, prepared teachers to teach each other, collaboratively, about approaches to teaching writing they have learned. After completing the Summer Institute, its members also become part of an ongoing network of teachers who meet, talk, write, and support one another as they continue learning on their own.

The title of the writing project is slightly misleading. Although the teaching of writing is at the core of what teachers learn from the project, it is done within the context of learning as a whole. Therefore, it crosses curriculum areas and addresses all aspects of what teaching and learning ought to be about. This is a bridge that is helping me bring together my vision of what democratic education should be and how to make it happen.

PRESSURES AFFECTING MY CLASSROOM PRACTICE

Sometimes, as a teacher, it's hard for me to stand up for what I really believe education should be. In my school, for example, particularly in the lower grades, I have felt pressure to conform to traditional reading practices.

Years ago our district adopted a basal series by Houghton Mifflin (1986a–f). We are expected to start with *Bells* (the beginning primer) in September, progress through *Drums* and *Trumpets*, followed by *Parades* (the first hardcover reading text), *Carousels*, and *Adventures*. "Don't skip stories or you'll miss crucial skills they'll need by second grade," the unspoken rule says.

The basals are, after all, scientifically researched by professionals with degrees who organize the skills that teachers will need to teach children in order for them to efficiently learn how to read. The organizational plan is then laid out in "Scope and Sequence" charts that demonstrate in what order teachers should teach each skill. Furthermore, in an effort to maximize efficiency and to ensure that the children are properly taught with the "most appropriate methods," based, of course, on empirical research, the authors and publishers of these basals provide teachers' guides with explicit directions in lesson-plan format "guiding" the teacher with "You say/They say" scripts. Not only do these scripts tell teachers what questions to ask their students, they also tell them word for word, paragraph by paragraph, what information to give students about the skill being taught. These are not, in fact, teachers' *guides*; they are teachers' *scripts*, intended for people with no knowledge of teaching.

That these so-called guides even exist is an insult to me. Yet, having been educated in much the same fashion from elementary through high school, I found myself falling back on these manuals, especially in my first year of teaching. Teachers around me talked to each other about what skills they were currently covering, which skills their students didn't understand, and which skills they were having to teach *now* because, apparently, "they didn't get it last year." The language they used didn't make it clear whose fault it was that the children didn't have those "prerequisite" skills, but I didn't want to be blamed or thought of as inadequate, especially since I was a beginning teacher.

Retreating into the basals at once relieved some of the pressure on me to "succeed" because I was now doing what my fellow teachers seemed to consider "teaching reading." If I followed the basals' Scope and Sequence charts and did the workbook pages specified in the teacher's guide, I would, it seemed, not be held accountable if the children didn't learn to read. The children themselves would be blamed, perhaps due to their inattentiveness or to an undiagnosed learning disability. In my case, teaching English as a Second Language, if students did not learn to read "at grade level," it was often believed to be because they were "language deficient" to begin with.

Although I was teaching children to read in a "professionally acceptable way," I continued to feel pressure. It was a self-imposed pressure that told me that I was teaching in a way completely unacceptable to the philosophy of education I'd researched and worked many hard years to construct for myself. My actual teaching was almost completely teacher-centered. It did not allow the students any input into deciding what or how something was taught. There was never any discussion about why we should learn what we were learning. Most questions I posed had only one right answer (which could be found in the teachers' manual). These questions rarely engaged students in meaningful discussions about the stories we read and almost never allowed them to make connections between what they read and their own lives. There was no chance for personal reflection or critical question-raising. My students become restless and bored, and so did I.

There is a lot of talk, within and outside of schools, about the need to hold teachers "accountable." This usually means that the public wants to be sure that teachers are producing desired learning outcomes from their students. There is a growing concern about our country's position in the global, economic marketplace (National Commission on Excellence in Education, 1983). We seem to be "losing the race in the workplace," and our work force is assumed to be at fault. The workers, it is believed, lack the education that our successful competitors have. Because "education" is deemed to be the answer to our economic woes, the public focuses on measurable (and comparable) educational outcomes, such as standardized test scores. Such tests are supposed to show what knowledge a child has or has not acquired. Knowledge, in this sense, is thought to be a static, impersonal, unchanging entity that is passed from teacher to student. The teacher teaches it; the student learns it. However, teaching and learning are not so clear-cut and simplistic.

Weren't my students learning as a result of the carefully sequenced stories and related skills in the basal series? Sure, they learned. They learned to look at their neighbor's workbook page because they couldn't rely on their own knowledge to generate the one correct answer. Even if they could generate the answer, they learned to stop taking risks because their self-confidence was low after having offered the wrong answer too many times. They learned that forgetting their pencil every day is better than bringing one. When supplied with a pencil, they learned that a broken pencil lead creates opportunities for extended trips to the pencil sharpener and a chance to socialize with others in their same predicament. They also learned that watching television is a whole lot more fun than reading a book any day of the week. Inadvertently, I had taught them all of these things as well as the worst lesson of all—that they could not be trusted, whatsoever, to direct their own learning, and that there was nothing of any real value in their own lives that they could contribute to our community of learners. I knew that my teaching had to change. But how?

CONSTRAINTS AFFECTING MY CLASSROOM PRACTICE

Aside from the pressures of traditional teaching I continue to feel, there are other constraints I face, particularly as an ESL teacher. As a resource teacher, each year I inevitably have scheduling difficulties. Since I don't have a self-contained classroom, I have to work with the other staff members to determine when I can take my students out of their classrooms.

Generally, I try to group my students by grade level and work with them during their Reading and Language Arts period. For example, one year I had first and second graders daily from 9:10 A.M. to 10:40 A.M. Then, from 10:45 A.M. to 12:15 P.M., I had third and fourth graders. Finally, from 1:00 P.M. to 2:30 P.M., I had fifth graders. It was the best schedule I ever experienced, having each group with me for 90 minutes. But even 90-minute class sessions can be too short, especially when attempting to provide time for democratic decision making and daily conflict resolution.

The following year the classroom schedules changed so that the first, second, and fourth grades all had reading at the same time. Some classes also shortened their reading periods to 60 minutes. Not only did my own class periods shorten, I also had to meet with the third and fourth grades separately, which added a "class" to my schedule. You can't fully appreciate what an extra class does to my schedule until you accompany me through a day to see all of the transitions that take place with different groups, at different grade levels, containing a wide variety of language levels as they come and go from my tiny classroom, with no time in between. These changes in class time have made it more difficult for me to take the time necessary to democratically make decisions or to resolve conflicts.

My classroom isn't "a classroom." As mentioned earlier, it's actually two office spaces combined. It is very small considering I have between 12 and 15 students in it at any one time. There's no room for desks, really, so I have two rectangular tables. Most of the time this means that my students are forced to sit elbow to elbow with their friends, and sometimes with their "enemies," too.

In our room, we live in a one-size-fits-all environment. My first graders swim at the tables that confine my fourth and fifth graders. We have no windows, since we are in the interior of the building—which makes it a challenge to study a unit on plant growth. One year I had to borrow window space from the room across the hall. Our plants had to get both water and sunlight from that room. We merely used our room to record the plants' daily growth. (I often seriously question the likelihood of our own growth, both physically and intellectually, in a room with no fresh air, no sunlight, no view of the outside world.) There are no countertops and no drawers in which to store materials. There are a few bookshelves, a metal cart on wheels (aka the art cart), an overhead projector on a cart, and three brown wooden boxes at our disposal for housing our books and materials. I even bought cardboard shoe organizers that double as student mailboxes where they can store their paper, pencils, and projects in progress (as long as they're small enough to fit). I try to keep all of these objects, except for the two rectangular tables, on the perimeter of the room so that we have floor space in which to enjoy storybook reading, together as a class or individually during silent reading time.

As much as I've tried, it is hard to make room for learning centers, listening centers, book-making areas, a writing center, and the like. We get in each other's way when we try to find space to work independently.

I have three or four classes each day. Sometimes, when we run out of time, one class ends up cleaning up the cookie dough that the other class has left behind, all the while demanding to know why they can't make it too. Again, one class's art mural often takes up floor space from another class while it dries. Space and time are constant constraints for most teachers and students, but particularly for us.

MY CLASSROOM PRACTICE IN TRANSITION

Like many teachers, I was afraid of "losing control." Especially in my first year, I wanted the principal to have a positive impression of me. I believed that if I tried implementing practices that allowed "too much" student choice or freedom, he would think I wasn't "doing my job." Even though I had heard how supportive this principal was, I didn't know him well personally at that time and I feared his evaluation of my work. My ego (and my sense of job security) was heavily dependent on his positive evaluation of my teaching. Even so, my heart was still dedicated to becoming a democratic teacher. It was the tension between "just surviving" as a teacher and becoming a democratic one that kept me searching and experimenting.

I started making changes gradually. One of the first attempts I made to establish democratic practices in my classroom was to make classroom rules with my first and second graders—at that time, the only group large enough to feel like a class. I asked them to brainstorm some possible rules we should have in our room. To my surprise, they had no trouble coming up with rules, such as: "No talking," "No running around the room," "No writing on the chalkboard without the teacher's permission," "No standing on the desks," "No fighting," "No chewing gum," "No eating food."

The brainstorming went on and on. Each suggestion usually followed the same format, starting with the word *no*. My students were obviously familiar with what *not* to do, but were unable to suggest what we *should* do. With some help, they came up with a few positive statements like, "Treat others the way you want them to treat you" and "Always ask before you borrow someone else's things."

When it came time to choose which rules would be included on a classroom chart to be displayed on the wall for the year, my commitment to the democratic process was put to the test. Arguments broke out. Each person who suggested a rule had a personal investment and had to see his or her rule make it to the classroom chart. After much discussion, the class concurred that they really didn't like it when a *lot* of rules were imposed on them. They were willing to let go of some rules with the understanding that they were good ones and that we'd abide by them anyway, but they didn't need a place on the chart.

We went on to generate a list of consequences ranging from reminders of what the rules were, to missing recess, to visiting the principal's office. I was never satisfied with our list, but the students were committed to it. They weren't angels but the rules took on new meaning because they, themselves, had created them. In fact, there seemed to be an unspoken consequence to this process, namely that students who broke the rules suffered the embarrassment of not being able to live up to their own words. When I called their attention to their behavior and pointed to their rules list, a special wave of guilt washed over their faces as their eyes hit the floor.

Another attempt I made at classroom democracy was engaging my third and fourth graders in dramatizing a play we had read. The language of the original text was a little more sophisticated than they were comfortable with, so I borrowed a computer from a regular classroom and had the students dictate their lines the way they wanted to say them. While some students worked with me on dictation, others were in charge of determining how many scenes we would have and what props we would need. The group worked for about one month on this project. We videotaped the final run-through and shared it with other classes. Most of the students proudly checked out the tape and took it home to share with their families. This experience allowed students to claim their own voice, as well as to make decisions that enhanced their sense of efficacy and autonomy. Both are important undertakings for students to develop if they are to take part in participatory decision making and to develop a sense of community.

Whenever there are group decisions to be made, the chance that disagreements will break out is great. But when students are faced with an abrupt end to a popular project about which they cannot work out their differences, complex negotiations begin to take place that are often surprising. These negotiations aren't always successful, of course. Sometimes I have to help sort out what the problems are. But sometimes I can't. The democratic process is nothing short of unpredictable.

Another attempt to foster democratic participation was initiated with my fourth graders last year. One day I announced that I would no longer call on them to speak. I said that part of learning to live and work together includes learning to be fair and to take turns. They were most uncomfortable with this process at first. For example, one day we were working on vocabulary words. They had to predict their meaning, find them in the dictionary, and then help produce what we called our "classroom definitions." I would say, "OK, the next word is 'determined.'" Right away, six or seven hands flew straight up in the air. I smiled and said, "Don't bother putting your hand in the air. It's not my decision who gets to speak." At first, without even a glance at anyone but me, they all began speaking at once. Then I'd say, "You can't all speak at once, can you? You're going to have to take turns." They thought about systematically going around in a circle, as they had done in other situations. They soon realized, however, that in this rigid structure, not everyone had something to contribute. Eventually, with a little coaching, they learned that the only way to *get* a turn when they wanted it was to be willing to *give* a turn sometimes.

Eventually I felt very gratified as I watched them eye one another to see who wanted to contribute before deciding together who should have that turn. They learned to be more patient with and considerate of each other. Although there were days when they bickered over nonsense, such as elbows touching as they sat at the table, overall, I was pleased with how they learned to get along. Working in pairs or in small groups also became easier for them as negotiating turn-taking became an expected activity accomplished without my involvement.

While each of these practices individually was important for me, I still lack what I consider democratic practices related specifically to the curriculum. What should I teach and how should I teach it? Why? Until now, I have either followed the district guidelines concerning what to teach, or ventured off on my own. But either way I have gone, I have not included the students in this decision-making process. In the future I want to begin incorporating them into this process by finding out what kinds of things they'd like to study. With a little imagination and creativity I should be able to incorporate the district's curriculum into our studies.

In the meantime, I am beginning to use what I've learned from my studies through the Chicago Area Writing Project. I believe, as do many researchers on the topic, that human beings have a deep need to write. Writing helps us make sense of our experiences and allows us to share parts of ourselves with others. If this is true, it means that writing is, in part, a deeply personal activity that becomes stifled if imposed on us from the outside. Therefore, it is crucial to not only allow but actually encourage my students to choose their own writing topics and to maintain ownership of their writing from beginning to end.

With most of my students, I have started what is called Writing Workshop. It is through Writing Workshop that I teach them the process of writing. Since most writers, amateur or professional, go through similar processes in order to successfully complete a piece of writing, I find it imperative to teach children how to do this. During Writing Workshop, they learn how to pre-write, draft, revise, edit, and publish their own work. They learn punctuation, capitalization, grammar, and word usage throughout the year in the context of their own work. They learn that the purpose of writing is to communicate and that the purpose of learning the mechanics of writing is to aid them in their communication.

Teaching writing through Writing Workshop is, for me, a practice in democracy. Students are encouraged to choose their own topics, which empowers them to find their personal voices. They begin to explore who they are, what they are interested in, and what they have to say. They learn to set goals for themselves and to become responsible for choosing the skills they need to learn in order to accomplish the writing they have set out to do. Students learn to give and receive constructive feedback, which puts them in the position of being teachers as well as students. Writing in this way is a very dynamic process and the progress students make is usually inspirational.

A colleague of mine taught me about Literature Circles. Right away I was drawn to the concept because of its cooperative design, which places the responsibility of reading and discussing a book in the hands of children. Ideally, there would be several small groups containing five or six students each. The groups could then choose their own book. Each member of each group is assigned a particular job. The jobs usually involve summarizing, vocabulary building, developing discussion questions, choosing passages to discuss, illustrating interesting or important scenes, and evaluating how well the group and its process are working.

I have created a literature circle with fourth graders. Although it was a challenge helping them learn how to do the different jobs, I have seen some very interesting results. When they read, they have a purpose beyond merely reading the words and declaring themselves "done" with the assignment. They are working much harder, trying to understand more fully what they are reading, because they want to have an interesting conversation about the story. Since they choose what questions they want to ask or what passages they want to discuss, they are more interested and invested in the book as well as the discussion of it. I see them making decisions constantly about what is important in the story and then, as a group, evaluating each other's choices compassionately, yet critically. This process shares some of the same democratic principles as Writing Workshop. The students are empowered as decision makers and are in control of the process with occasional guidance from the teacher. They are learning to think critically about their work and how to evaluate it. These are several of the qualities they need to develop to be creative problem solvers and democratic citizens.

CONCLUSION

Coming to understand what democracy means (or *can* mean) and how to make it come alive, especially in my classroom, has been anything but simple. My understanding of it is evolving. I believe I am making significant strides toward becoming a more democratic teacher, but I also realize that I have much more to learn.

Although I have faced and continue to face certain pressures and constraints as a teacher, I am deeply committed to a vision that values democracy as a major aim of educating our youth. I was fortunate to have begun my teaching career with a supportive, democratic principal and several colleagues who share many of my principles. Yet, it is my curiosity that continues to push me. It tells me there is a lot I don't yet know about teaching and learning. This curiosity is my strength because it doesn't allow me to be completely satisfied with my current teaching practice. It will push me to continue building bridges, prompting me to cross over them and back as many times as it takes to lead me to a more democratic practice.

NOTE

1. Elmore A. Johnson is the principal about whom I am speaking. He was my principal during my first three years of teaching, from 1990 to 1993. After retiring in July 1993, he fell ill and passed away December 22, 1993. I wish to dedicate this chapter to his memory, for many reasons. Elmore had faith in my ability to "find my own way" when I was just beginning teaching. Not only did he have endless faith in my ability to learn and grow, but he also had the patience to wait for me to come to him for advice. In fact, he kept insisting that I be more patient with myself by telling me, "Rome wasn't built in a day, Noelle." His faith, patience, and encouragement kept me from self-destructing (quite literally) during that crucial first year and has helped me become the confident risk-taker that I am today and will continue to be. Thank you, Elmore!

REFERENCES

Barber, B. (1984). *Strong Democracy*. Berkeley: University of California Press.
Bellah, R. N., Madsen, R., Sullivan, W. M., Swidler, A., & Tipton, S. M. (1985). *Habits of the heart: Individualism and commitment in American life*. Berkeley: University of California Press.

Houghton Mifflin. (1986a). *Bells*. Boston: Houghton Mifflin.
Houghton Mifflin. (1986b). *Drums*. Boston: Houghton Mifflin.
Houghton Mifflin. (1986c). *Trumpets*. Boston: Houghton Mifflin.
Houghton Mifflin. (1986d). *Parades*. Boston: Houghton Mifflin.
Houghton Mifflin. (1986e). *Carousels*. Boston: Houghton Mifflin.
Houghton Mifflin. (1986f). *Adventures*. Boston: Houghton Mifflin.
National Commission on Excellence in Education. (1983). *A nation at risk: The imperative for educational reform*. Washington, DC: U.S. Government Printing Office.
Webster's Intermediate Dictionary. (1977). G. & C. Merriam Company.

SIX

Creating a Democratic Classroom: Empowering Students Within and Outside School Walls

Krista Sorensen

In order to be successful, it is important that teachers establish a vision of the ideal classroom. What is the tone of the classroom? What is the role of the teacher? What curriculum will be explored, what teaching methodologies will be used, and how will global issues be addressed? What philosophy of education is most appropriate? In addition, and in conjunction with one's philosophy of education, teachers must have a more integrated vision that encompasses social, economic, and political views. These two visions cannot be isolated—social ideals and perspectives are reflected in teaching practices, and educational ideals will be intertwined with problems, issues, and events in society. It is interesting, then, how the culture of schooling has often served to keep these two realms separate, to teach curriculum as isolated subjects, and to keep teachers' personal perspectives and values stifled, and questions of ideology excluded (Beyer, 1989).

My vision of an ideal classroom centers on creating a democratic environment where students are given the opportunity for empowerment. Before I describe my own attempts at creating a democratic classroom, it is first necessary to explore the meaning and the implications of the term empowerment.

Empowerment has become a buzzword in contemporary educational circles. Teachers and scholars have spent a good deal of time discussing issues surrounding teacher and student empowerment (e.g., see Beyer, 1991a). Much of this language is present in school reform literature that discusses, among other complex topics, the need for autonomy in schools.

Not unlike much of the educational jargon that is freely tossed around, the term itself and its importance are often reduced to a mere slogan; it is simplified and trivialized. However, the possibilities of genuine empowerment offer significant and complex avenues for school restructuring. There must be sincere, in-depth dialogue about the importance of teacher, student, and parent empowerment and their interrelationships.

Because I am a teacher committed to creating an atmosphere in which students are given the opportunity for empowerment, the environment or ethos of my classroom is shaped by a larger philosophy of education. In order to have a classroom that is conducive to meaningful learning, several things must occur. First, the teacher must have a vision of what empowerment means and how empowerment can be promoted in the classroom. This vision is an ideal, which will change through teacher reflection and experience. Second, an environment must be created that is non-threatening and encourages participants (both students and teachers) to be risk-takers. Respect for each other's ideas is critical. Knowledge must be seen by all as something that is valuable, exciting, and constructed out of an experience involving each of the participants. The reason many students do not take risks is that they have not been given the freedom or autonomy to do so. They have not been taught to think critically and challenge ideas, and they are looking to please the teacher with the "right answer." Teachers, too, look to please administrators by following standardized curriculum and testing activities without trying more progressive ideas and methodologies.

Establishing an open, non-threatening classroom environment allows teachers and students to share the ownership of knowing. This also enables teachers to relinquish the strain of artificially imposed authority that, because of the hidden curriculum and the hierarchical structure of schools, is present in many classrooms. This idea of sharing the ownership of knowing is key to the possibilities for student empowerment. In a traditional classroom, students are often taught to passively accept knowledge presented by external authorities, such as teachers or textbooks. Information presented to the student is not always meaningful because it has not been discovered by the student and little critical reflection is involved. Students do not feel a sense of ownership or accomplishment when factual information is merely "fed" to them. In a classroom where students are striving for empowerment, an entirely different process and experience is taking place. Students are making decisions, reflecting on and evaluating experiences, thinking critically—and they are given the time and support to do so. Answers, then, do not come from external authorities such as teachers or texts, but from the students themselves. Knowledge is actively pursued through classroom dialogue, interaction, and discussion. This shared participation in the generation of knowledge allows for learners to begin to construct their own meanings about complex questions and issues. In turn, the social fabric of the classroom is further strengthened. Empowerment involves knowledge that is genuine and comes from sharing experiences, ideas, perspectives, and values with others. This shared ownership between teacher and student is exciting because students are no longer regurgitating passively acquired information. In addition, students do not have to "prove" to the teacher that they have mastered the "given material" for a class. Instead, knowledge is created, shared, and respected by all involved.

CREATING A DEMOCRATIC CLASSROOM ENVIRONMENT

Contrary to misunderstandings about the nature of a democratic classroom—one that promotes freedom, decision making, risk-taking, and group participation—a classroom of this sort is not without structure. In fact, the teacher has a vital if difficult role in guiding the development of a democratic classroom. Without a teacher's vision and experience, a democratic classroom cannot be created.

Students, through no fault of their own, do not always come to us ready to think critically, reflect on issues, make decisions, solve problems cooperatively, and feel a sense of ownership of knowledge. I have found that I must actually demonstrate and teach these activities to my students. Children are naturally inquisitive and curious; however, the hierarchical structure of schools, as well as experiences outside classrooms, often socialize them into becoming passive receptors of external information, "facts," and values.

Teaching students to be empowered starts with a non-threatening classroom environment. At the beginning of the year, my students and I spend a lot of time creating and establishing our classroom environment. We get to know each other's needs and interests through lots of cooperative group work and small-group and class discussions. It is important that my students respect and value the knowledge of their classmates. All students have unique voices and experiences to bring to the classroom. All students have special talents to share. As we work to form a community of learners, it is important to get to know each other as human beings. Through activities such as cooperative learning, peer tutoring, peer editing, cooperative researching, and the sharing of creative writing, poetry, and literature, students begin to see the value of peer input and collaboration in the learning process.

At the beginning of the year we establish classroom rules together. At first this is very difficult because students want to give all the school rules they have previously memorized and internalized:

> "No running or talking in the halls."
> "No talking when the teacher is talking."
> "Raise your hand if you want to answer a question."
> "Don't talk back."

Usually I do not write down their initial responses. The class quickly, without much thought, rattles off about 25 rules. The next step is to get the students thinking about these rules. I ask the class, "Why do you think we have rules?" Typical responses include the following:

> Alan, the quiet boy and passive learner: "Because."
> Sally, the overachiever: "So we can learn."
> Maria, the teacher-pleaser: "Because the teacher/principal says so."
> Joshua, the self-proclaimed class clown: "Who knows?"

Realizing my need to probe further, I ask more specific questions: "Is there ever a time when it is okay to run or talk in the hall? Why is it not good to talk when the teacher is talking? Why should we raise our hands? Do we always have to? What does it mean to talk back? How can you express your feelings and frustrations without being disrespectful to each other?" We usually have an in-depth discussion that requires significant time and energy. I try to do more listening and let the students form the direction of the conversation. But, especially at the beginning of the year, there are often major silences in the discussion, with 30 pairs of eyes staring directly at me for direction or confirmation. However, when we have finished this process as a class, we have created a statement shaped by our participation in a democratic process. It is one that guides our classroom environment and serves as discipline policy for accountability-driven administrators and parents. Agreeing that learning is a main goal of school, our statement is usually something like: DO NOT DISTURB THE LEARNING OF OTHERS or HELP OTHERS LEARN. On reflection, nearly all "traditional" classroom rules will fall under this category. Fighting, swearing, and interrupting will indeed disturb the learning of others. Being disrespectful, teasing, or not valuing others' opinions will not help us learn. At another time, I will have the class divide into small groups and discuss ways to implement our "motto." This helps make the information more concrete, and enables the students to actually put it into action. Our rules, then, become meaningful, and students are able to actively acknowledge their importance.

Learning and the pursuit of knowledge are first and foremost in the minds of the students. I have even heard my kindergartners say to each other, "Carol, you are disturbing my learning." When we make classroom activities enjoyable, relevant, and meaningful, students value learning and see its importance.

Parents can easily be engaged in this process by communicating to them the importance of creating a school structure that is centered around establishing a classroom of learners. As children understand this concept and put it into practice, they become messengers. Most parents, if their children are excited about the classroom environment, will also be supportive. It feels good to receive notes from parents saying, "My child has never been this excited about school. Keep up the good work." Teachers do not always get a lot of parental support, so notes like this really help to reinforce your goals and vision for the class. Although creating rules or expectations together as a class is a seemingly basic procedure that many teachers do, it is one important component in creating a foundation for student empowerment.

Empowering Students Through a Democratic Classroom

Decision making, critical thinking, reflection, and recognizing multiple viewpoints are all part of the process of empowerment. However, empowerment cannot be achieved without action. That is why it is so important that students experience learning on a firsthand basis and be actively engaged in the learning and evaluation process. The subject at hand must be something that is meaningful and significant to students. Wasting time on trivial curricular topics and spending time on insignificant issues instead of vital problems in the real world demean the students and the teacher. Empowerment involves action; action involves change. Empowered individuals work to make meaningful changes to benefit their community.

Thus, the classroom environment I strive to create is one in which learning is meaningful and significant in my students' lives, and knowledge is actively gained rather than passively received. My classroom environment must provide opportunities for discourse, so that students can listen, discuss, debate, and come to their own conclusions on issues. My classroom environment encourages critical thinking and reflection, while providing a safety net for students to try new ideas, perhaps fail, but then feel supported and confident enough to try again. The ideas of everyone (students and teachers) are respected, and knowledge is seen as something valuable and exciting. Students understand that they can act on this knowledge to make changes in society. Students truly believe that they have the power to know; that knowledge is power.

Empowering Students Through Thematic Teaching

Learning will be most meaningful and most successful when students can identify with the problem or issue at hand. Therefore, it is important for me to allow them to have input into the selection of curriculum and in the evaluation process. Thematic teaching has been very successful in my classroom, partially because it allows children to explore issues holistically and gain a broader perspective. When teaching is done thematically, teachers are able to share the reality of the interconnected nature of the world with students through the curriculum. When different subject areas are linked, learning is more meaningful.

For example, our theme for 1992–1993 was the Earth. Students quickly found how encompassing environmental issues are as we read books and articles about environmental issues during reading time, included the relevant vocabulary on our spelling test, wrote letters to various people and groups expressing some of our concerns, and calculated and graphed the amount of waste created in the United States. We also did experiments on biodegradable substances. At the beginning of the year the class chose 12 different pieces of trash (articles such as paper, glass, aluminum, and yard waste). We made predictions about which substances were and were not biodegradable, and we recorded our predictions. We then buried the materials outside. At the end of May we uncovered the materials and checked our findings against our predictions. During the year we also looked at the history of environmental problems and at how pollution is significantly affecting different countries. My fourth graders became very interested in the ozone problem and its effects in countries such as Chile and Australia. We devoted a significant amount of time to extra reading and research on this issue. I had planned to briefly mention the ozone problem in a lesson on air pollution. The students had so many questions and concerns that my intended five-minute discussion lasted almost five days! The same thing happened in our discussion of endangered animal species. The students really became attached to this issue and were soon on personal campaigns to stop the sale of fur coats and the destruction of rain forests. The students were making decisions regarding the direction of their learning. They were thinking critically about important global issues, and they were expanding their own knowledge through the collective efforts of their peers. Their interests sparked me to do a comprehensive thematic unit on rain forests. I brought in outside resources; we learned about the rain forests' role in weather patterns, medicines, herbs, and foods. Through different projects we explored the wonderful diversity of rain forests. Students were always bringing in new resources they found at home or in the library. By the end of the year, they were walking, talking resources on rain forests. I had learned a great deal from them, and they worked hard to transform our classroom into a rain forest. Using the knowledge we had gained from our studies, our class constructed a very detailed and factually specific rain forest. Various features of the rain forest were evident; different layers of the terrain, distinct herbs, medicines, and leaves were present; native animals and insects flourished; and an impressive level of detail was put into capturing the diversities of a tropical rain forest. On the second to last day of school, after many previous requests to take down our rain forest, I was still confronted with anguished voices crying, "Please Mrs. Sorensen, please don't cut down and destroy the rain forest."

Our environmental theme was very interesting and meaningful to students. They felt responsible for doing something because it was significant to them and they realized that these issues would affect their world. For students, the chance to reach out of the classroom context and touch reality is exciting. The classroom is the perfect place to initiate this process because they know it is safe.

Empowering students cannot occur in only one area or during one part of the day. Writing is an important area where students should have control. We use Writing Workshop each day in the classroom, giving students the opportunity to write about topics and issues that are meaningful to them. They can write individually or in groups. They work at their own pace to brainstorm, create a rough draft, go through the process of editing, and then, if they wish, publish their writing. The published work is then displayed in the classroom library and shared with other students. Peer interaction is an important component of this process. It has become a habit for many students to rely on approval and advice from adults concerning their work. Peers have valuable ideas and knowledge that must not be ignored. Writing can be very empowering; however, many teachers still complain that their students "don't like to write." To avoid this, writing must be meaningful, real, and identifiable. When writers produce a wonderful piece of writing, it is most likely because they have written about something that is significant in their lives. Often, as a result, readers are touched by this writing because so many life experiences can be related to those of others—regardless of age, race, gender, religion, or ethnicity. It is important to give authors control and ownership of their work. Although teachers or other students may offer advice and suggestions, the ultimate decisions about writing are left to the author. Through this process, students continue to become empowered and take responsibility for their own learning.

While it is becoming more common to involve students in the learning process, they must also be involved in the process of evaluation. Reflective portfolios are something that I started using during the 1994–1995 school year. I view portfolios as a collection of work that shows growth. These portfolios do not contain meaningless pieces of paper, but instead collections that indicate student learning and growth. The purpose of these portfolios is to celebrate that growth. Portfolios are used for self-reflection by each child about her or his own process of learning. During the year, students must periodically go through their portfolios and reflect on the progress they have made. Reflection is the most important part of this process. It must be a collaborative effort by the student, the teacher, and the parents. Reflecting on their work is a high-level thinking activity that should be practiced in all areas of learning. Reflective portfolios may be used in all curriculum areas.

Being part of the evaluation process, I believe, will help students feel ownership of the process of becoming knowledgeable. Students are able to control their own learning because they are involved in creating expectations so they have a very clear picture of what must be accomplished and how that will be done. In addition, self-assessment will illustrate to students that grading is not an arbitrary act that is done "to them." Instead, it is a tool for growth. In *Portfolios: Stories of Knowing*, Paulson and Paulson (1991) nicely describe portfolios. "A portfolio," they say, "tells a story. It is the story about knowing" (p. 2). It is exciting that through portfolios students can tell their own stories of learning.

Decision Making

A democratic classroom must provide a consistent environment for students throughout the day. Students must know that this environment will always be present. As a teacher, it is my job to guarantee that this environment persists. Therefore, in all I do, I try to give students opportunities for input and decision making. Decision making is a necessary component of a democratic classroom. Because of the numerous situations that arise during the day demanding some type of decision making involving human interaction, decision making is a seemingly natural part of all classrooms. Every day, hundreds of decisions, on a variety of levels, are made in classrooms by teachers and students. Decisions are made by the teacher from as small as "Should I let Anthony go to the bathroom—again?" or "Whose cooperative group would Carlos best fit in?" to as big as "Does Emily have a learning disability?" or "Is David being physically abused at home—and what action do I take to confirm or refute my strong suspicions?" Students, too, are making decisions such as "Which book should I choose?" or "I forgot my homework, what should I tell the teacher?" or "Other children are treating me unfairly, what do I do?" Teachers must take advantage of the many problems and conflicts that arise throughout the day to allow students to make decisions themselves, and give them ample time and direction to sort through problems that are complex but significant to them.

The area of social problems is an appropriate place to begin encouraging decision making, especially with younger students. Many students are used to being told what to do. They are not allowed to solve problems or make decisions themselves. Teachers can start small and demonstrate this decision-making process for them. At the beginning of the year, I encourage students to solve problems on the playground. Together, we brainstorm options for solving these problems. As the year progresses, I expand their decision-making abilities by allowing them to pick options for work, activities, and projects, or to choose literature and curriculum. I also like to incorporate decision making into the evaluation processes. I will ask students to reflect on and respond to their own papers or a peer's work, or select materials to put into their portfolio. When selecting materials for their portfolio it is important for the students to reflect on and critique their work. "Why did you choose this piece, why do you feel it is your best, most meaningful or most creative work?"

Of course, there are some areas in which I am not empowered to give students freedom—for example, in changing certain state- or district-mandated curricula. In these circumstances, I encourage student input in formulating ideas, activities, or projects we could do to learn about the pre-established curriculum. Even in the worst-case scenarios, some type of student input is appropriate and possible. For example, I can not very well ask students *if* they would like to take the Iowa Test of Basic Skills or the Illinois Goals Assessment Program, or if there is any way we should *change* these tests. All classes must follow rigorous and admittedly agonizing routines in the administration of these standardized tests. Yet, despite the students' and my lack of control over the testing procedures and the content of the test itself, it is necessary to allow time to critique and discuss this procedure.

Schools and Society

The creation of a democratic classroom that allows for student empowerment has the exciting potential to go beyond the school doors. Ideals from a democratic classroom can be transferred into larger social contexts through the active participation of students. Whether this happens leads us back to two conflicting historical questions in education: Do schools serve as programs to maintain social homogeneity and social control, or do schools serve as agents of change that adjust to the needs of our pluralistic society and the need for social justice? Historically, those in positions of power have said yes to social control and no to pluralism. However, some teachers have said, and continue to say, no to social homogeneity and yes to social reconstruction. School and society cannot and do not function independently. Each one of my students embodies unique characteristics that make her or him special and important. Each student brings unique problems into the classroom that can often be attributed or linked to factors or problems in society. And, each student will become an adult, participating in social, cultural, economic, environmental, and political activities of one sort or another.

For example, many of my students come from unstable and dysfunctional families. By dysfunctional I do not necessarily mean "non-traditional," because recent studies point out that "traditional" families with two married parents accounted for only 56% of all households in 1989 (Rubin and Borgers, 1991, p. 11). Instead, I mean homes where there are alcoholic, abusive, neglectful, non-supportive or poverty-stricken parents. Changing social dynamics also create realities such as single-parent homes, high divorce rates, teenage pregnancies, and gang involvement, which have major implications for our classrooms. Children coming to us frequently bring with them horrible experiences and emotional difficulties. Students bring this "baggage" with them into the classroom, and this will necessarily affect teaching and learning. Yet, regardless of these outside factors, it is my responsibility, as a teacher, to try to reach these students. For many who come from troubled homes, teachers are perceived as the most stable aspects of their wider environments.

Language and cultural biases also can get in the way of effective learning and student empowerment. Students who are taught English at an early age in school can lose fluency in their native language, thus jeopardizing family relations and communications at home. This is detrimental to both the parents, who feel disconnected from their children and disempowered in their new country, and for children, who are losing important guidance and communication with their parents and losing a sense of cultural identity and belonging. Members of some families report being unable to communicate with one another when children switch to English. Although most families want their children to learn English, because they know it is critical to their economic survival in this country, the breakdown of communication between parents and children interrupts normal family and social dynamics, alienates those involved, and does not allow meaningful knowledge, expertise, and culture to be transmitted from one generation to the next.

The interrelations between schooling and society are real and continuous. What we teach in school can have a major impact on society. And, as we all know too well, society has a major impact on what we teach in school. Henry Giroux (1989), in "Rethinking Education Reform in the Age of George Bush," asks these questions: "What kind of society do we want? How do we educate students for a truly democratic society? What conditions must we provide for both teachers and students for such an education to be meaningful and workable?" (p. 729).

DEFINING DEMOCRACY

There is an important, prior question that must be addressed in terms of working for democratic education: What is the meaning of democracy? Certainly it is not the same for everyone. In our "democratic" country, U.S. citizens do not all view democracy in the same way. The American Dream, for many, seems to represent a belief that all people are capable of becoming free, independent, autonomous, financially well-off, and socially mobile. Individual competition is the way to succeed; the more independent you are (especially financially), the better. The American Dream for many includes looking out for yourself and your family, and working hard to get ahead and be independent. The American Dream often includes, as well, narrow electoral or political connotations. Maxine Greene (1988) suggests that Americans are indeed being continually polarized, maintaining individualistic, self-sufficient, independent, and autonomous attitudes concerning freedom. These attitudes and misconceptions about freedom are responsible for a growing apathy—in the nation as a whole—regarding social welfare, communal involvement, and general concern for global issues (Bellah, Madsen, Sullivan, Swidler, & Tipton, 1985).

In contrast to this individualistic notion of democracy, I support and seek to assist in developing a more global and participatory view of democracy and freedom. This definition goes beyond economic freedom to empowerment, social justice, and equality for members of society. This definition of democracy is in many ways parallel to the kind of democracy I strive to establish in my classroom. The focus here is not on individual freedoms, but instead on group participation. However, I don't think the two need be mutually exclusive, since individual freedom should and can occur within the context of community values and social rights. This understanding of democracy involves dialogue. It involves listening, discussing, debating, and acting. Individual empowerment, then, is created through the process of group participation and taking action towards change.

In *The Dialectic of Freedom*, Greene (1988) supports this notion of democracy and freedom, stressing that critical perspectives evoke meaningful thought and dialogue, giving people the desire to speak their own voice. Thus, those not engaged in critical inquiry are "unlikely to search for the spaces where they can come together to establish a 'sphere of freedom' (Arendt, 1958, p. 30), involving them in their plurality" (Greene, 1988, p. 3). Freedom, then, is viewed as an "opening of spaces"—a nice contrast to more commonly held beliefs of freedom as mandating independent and isolated autonomy. Most importantly, the opening of spaces Greene refers to depends on the actions we undertake, "the praxis we learn to devise" (Greene, 1988, p. 5).

George Wood (1988) also discusses alternative conceptions of democracy that deviate from standard views:

> An alternative, "strong" or "participatory" conception of democracy focuses upon public participation as opposed to representation. This classical notion has posited that democracy, in the words of John Dewey, "is more than a form of government; It is primarily a mode of associated living, of conjoint communicated experiences." That is, democracy is a way of living in which we collectively deliberate over shared problems and prospects. It is conceived as a system in which decisions are made by those who will be directly affected by the decision. (p. 169)

Creating and modeling a true democratic environment in the classroom can, I believe, lead to changes in society. But students must be taught to be reflective and to think globally, critically, and compassionately. If students are not challenged to participate in the gaining of knowledge and the real possibilities for learning in school, they will very likely become citizens who neglect social responsibility. In addition, Giroux (1989) suggests that ideals of global tolerance that will influence society should be initiated in the classroom: "A curriculum that respects the diversity of student voice also provides a referent for the principle of democratic tolerance as an essential condition of social life in a democracy" (p. 730). Creating a classroom in which students have a voice and can use that voice to make a difference is important. These will be the students and citizens who can look at issues globally and will act to make positive changes in society.

TEACHER, STUDENT, AND PARENT EMPOWERMENT: SOLUTIONS AND LIMITATIONS

In order to empower students, teachers first must be empowered. Recent reform literature supports the ideal of teacher leadership and participation in school decision making involving curriculum, instruction, testing, and policy (Beyer, 1991b, 1993; Goodman, 1992). Teachers and teacher education programs are being targeted as key elements in educational reform (Goodlad, 1984). By listening to teacher's voices and engaging teachers in dialogue about the problems and possibilities for school-ing, empowerment will occur for teachers and their students.

Teachers must act to make changes in schools and explore issues of teacher empowerment. What better source than teachers to gain theoreti-cal and practical insights on the most successful ways to educate lifelong learners? Nonetheless, there are numerous barriers present in the current structure of schools that greatly limit a teacher's ability to make changes.

The hierarchical structure of schools, the nature of the teaching force, and societal attitudes about teachers work against teacher autonomy and empowerment. The issue of gender is significant here in exploring com-ponents of teacher leadership, decision making, and the current structure of schools. Educational decisions about curriculum, discipline, and policy have traditionally been made by male administrators. This hierarchical structure of schools is not accidental. Historically, teachers (especially at the elementary level) have been women. Administrators have been men. Decisions have been made by administrators; instructions have been fol-lowed by teachers (Hoffman, 1981).

Over the last 150 years, there have been significant changes in the educational philosophy guiding schools. Prior to that time, the focus of education was within the family. Informal schooling took place in the home, given by mothers and grandmothers. During the 19th century, however, great shifts occurred in the way society viewed the purposes of education. Schools were now viewed as institutions that instill moral values and keep up with the demands imposed by modern industrialism. Women, "natu-rally," were seen as the people to properly instill these values and proper character traits in children (Hoffman, 1981).

This major transformation of society, in fact, had created a new "pro-fession" for women. The responsibility of inculcating moral values, coupled with the "need" for men to occupy more prestigious positions, lies at the heart of the current status of teachers. The limited degree of respectabil-ity and professionalism that is often attributed to educators, especially at the elementary level, comes from the presumption that teaching is a "woman's profession," and is tied to pervasive sexism in the society at large.

With the historical development of a new "profession for women" came the need to further educate women to fill the duties previously per-formed by men. In the mid-1800s the first normal schools were created to further educate and possibly professionalize women educators. Yet, because the normal schools were run by men, and because of gender-based social inequality, sexist attitudes and practices were apparent, and women were passively trained to fulfill objectives created by men running the normal schools. Teachers were often not allowed to take part in the deci-sion-making process or to have any ownership in or control over the materials they taught. Moreover, the negative effects of the normal schools, which served as a foundation for teacher training programs, are still apparent in our schools today.

Teachers, who are still mostly female, have been conditioned to accept white, middle-class, male-oriented curricula and organizational patterns. They have been taught to follow district guidelines and not challenge the system. Educators, and more specifically women educators, have not readily been allowed or encouraged to think critically or to act on issues of pedagogy and curriculum. Teachers do not often realize the potential strength they have to influence educational reform. The inferior position of especially working-class women in both schools and society has had an overwhelming effect on issues of teacher autonomy and empowerment. Many of these attitudes are still deeply instilled within educators and will be difficult to change. Nevertheless, such changes must be undertaken. Starting in teacher education programs and continuing in the schools themselves, teachers must be allowed real opportunities to actively be involved in formulating educational change.

In addition to the confining structure of schools, teachers have traditionally been restrained from making educational decisions and changes by the mandate for standardized testing, district- and statewide curriculum requirements, and our nation's obsession with quantitative accountability. A good deal of pressure is placed on teachers at my school to have their students do well on state standardized tests administered each year. The pressure comes from many sources: superintendents, principals, teachers, and parents, who want proof that teachers are successfully educating our children. Teachers themselves want their students to score well on achievement tests, as it is one measure of success that is taken seriously. Even if teachers do not value these tests, others in the community rely heavily on their results. In our district, test scores are printed in the newspaper and compared with those of other schools in the area, state, and nation. Each school completes a building report card that is sent home with each child. The superintendent even brings our district's scores to meetings to compare the results for different schools within our district. As much as teachers may try to downplay the significance of test scores and recognize the biases present within them, they are used as a major, and sometimes the only, source of evaluating teachers in the district.

Bureaucratic Limitations

As an ESL/bilingual teacher, I encountered many bureaucratic limitations that had to do with the specific bilingual program operating in our district and the attitudes and feelings that accompanied it. There were prejudices toward the Hispanic population on the part of district educators, administrators, and community members. There were many political limitations, restrictions, and unfair practices and procedures placed on the bilingual program and its students and teachers.

The structure of the bilingual program, specifically, often hindered educational practices. The primary grades, in recent years, had moved to a self-contained model that was indeed more successful. However, the intermediate students were involved in a half-day pull-out program that was set up for the children to fail. My fourth-grade students came to me in the afternoon. They were bussed to my school from five other elementary schools, thus wasting necessary teaching time. The students' day was very fragmented. Often they would have to leave the regular classroom in the middle of a project to come to the bilingual classroom. Also, the students were always rushed at lunch because they had to catch the bus. Because of the segmentation of the day, it was very difficult for some students to identify with a homeroom. In a democratic classroom a sense of community, trust, and belonging is crucial. Student empowerment occurs only when people are communicating and working together to share knowledge and experience.

In our district, I felt a lack of support for the bilingual program. This included insufficient support services for bilingual students such as teacher aides, school psychologists, and social workers. There were few bilingual translators to help facilitate parent-teacher communication, to discuss special evaluations, and to identify medical needs. In addition, the district had a large bilingual program, but did not have a specific bilingual coordinator. While the assistant superintendent of student support services was in charge of the bilingual program, her many other responsibilities made that responsibility overwhelming. In addition, her professional expertise is not in bilingual education. Because there was no bilingual coordinator to provide expertise in this area, sometimes communication was vague, and there was no consistent philosophy of bilingual education. Not only were philosophies inconsistent, but little or no time was provided for bilingual educators to collaborate, discuss the program, pose and solve problems, and exchange ideas and experiences.

Parents are not often involved in the bilingual program. They are not well informed or educated about school procedures, policies, curriculum, and philosophy. Language differences create a huge barrier. Hispanic parents' voices are often not heard; they, too, lack empowerment. There are no Hispanic administrators and few Hispanic teachers and role models in the school. The bureaucratic structure of the school system dictates that many restrictions are imposed that specifically affect bilingual programs.

Financial Limitations

Finally, in terms of limitations, funding is most often at the heart of discussions of educational problems and reform. Grants and funding are not equitably distributed; poorer or inner-city districts usually spend a fraction of what students in wealthy or middle-class suburban districts receive (Kozol, 1991). Questions about how much government funding should be available and to whom the funding should go, as well as what alternative sources of revenue could be tapped to provide suitable school environments for all students, must be continually addressed collectively by teachers, administrators, and community members.

Inequitable funding is an issue in all areas of education. Must this inequity persist? We are, in many respects, the world's wealthiest nation, and yet we do not seem to have the educational funding that other nations provide for their students. The problem is not money; it is making education a national priority. In *The Good Society*, Bellah and his colleagues (1991) discuss the definition of a genuine "educational society." They describe this type of society as requiring more than just good schools. An educational society must value morality, culture, and public spirit, and work toward the common good. The authors stress that although schools can contribute to needed social change, "only a further democratic transformation of all our institutions will make possible a genuine 'educational society'" (Bellah, Madsen, Sullivan, Swidler, & Tipton, 1991, p. 176).

CREATING DEMOCRATIC SCHOOLS

There is no easy-to-follow recipe for democracy. Individuals must share their knowledge, experience, and power in the struggle for democracy in our schools and in society. Instituting democracy in a genuinely participatory sense in classrooms will help propel broader social changes. A form of democracy involving ideals of global tolerance, participation, and critical reflection and action must be initiated in the classroom. Democratic schools are created by first establishing a vision for democratic education and student empowerment, and then by each educator's putting this vision into practice through teacher, student, and parental collaboration and participation.

There are countless barriers faced by educators on a daily basis. What must occur, then, for teachers to move past these barriers and realize their participatory role in educational and social reform? Of course, some structural and material changes must occur. Teachers must be given more autonomy when it comes to decision making and policy. More professional time must be allotted for teacher growth, and the general conditions of schools must be improved. Fewer bureaucratic restrictions and less mandatory completion of "secretarial" tasks would free teachers to do more "teaching." But beyond these material changes, some important ideological changes must occur if we are to empower teachers. Teacher participation and collaboration are at the heart of this issue. Increasing teacher autonomy will not ensure change. Teachers must be allowed to think critically and analytically, and to be actively involved in the pursuit of change.

A starting point for this transformation is in teacher education programs. These programs should combine teaching skills and strategies with a critical awareness that will help teachers be successful. Educators must be able to make decisions concerning curriculum and pedagogy and to elaborate on and communicate their educational vision. However, all too often, once teachers get "in the classroom," their ability to make educational decisions dissolves. This is where teacher collaboration and participation are crucial. Teachers must work together to make their voices heard. Maeroff (1988), in an article aimed at teacher empowerment, states that "ideally, collegiality will lead teachers and administrators to work together as partners and to share power. No longer should teachers have to become principals to influence policy" (p. 477).

Often we think of collaboration as being limited to sharing curricular ideas and teaching strategies. Yet this is only the beginning. Teachers must share ideas, knowledge, philosophies, ideologies, and experiences. Knowledge is not limited to facts; factual information is only at the surface of knowledge. Knowledge involves dialogue, reflection, and experience. I believe that one of the greatest sources of knowledge for a teacher is built on the sharing of experiences with colleagues. Teachers, through the sharing of ideas and experience, build on and expand their knowledge— knowledge that is real, valuable, and reflective and that leads to empowerment. Creating teacher networks is a necessary part of empowering teachers. Networks offer a place where meaningful dialogue will occur, systems will be critiqued, and solutions will be posed.

The collaboration that occurs between teachers must also occur between teachers and parents. Teachers realize that the most successful student learning occurs when students, parents, and educators work together toward the common goal of educating children. I try to involve parents as much as possible in the educational process and daily routine of our classroom. I send home weekly newsletters and student journals to keep families updated on events in our classroom. I make positive phone calls and send postcards to the parents of several students each week.

Parents are always welcome to come visit our classroom and participate in our activities. I often ask parents to come into the classroom or share information through their child about their culture, country, or areas of expertise. We had some wonderful presentations on Chinese New Year, Mexican Independence Day, origami, native dress of Laos, Russian churches, and Polish landscape and architecture. At the end of the year we have an ESL picnic when all families are invited to the school to share an ethnic dish. The children prepare information on the different cultures in the class through books, plays, flags, and presentations. It is a grand occasion and a learning experience for all.

This ongoing process of communication is important to the environment of our class. I learn a lot from parents about their children, their families, and their culture. Families are eager to share information, and I would be foolish not to capitalize on this opportunity. I have had some very enlightening and intellectual conversations with parents concerning political, educational, and economic issues. One of the conversations I treasure most was a two-hour discussion with Russian parents on the political situation in their home country.

Empowered teachers are at the heart of educational reform because they have the ability to influence others. By creating a democratic environment, they can empower students. When teachers involve parents in schooling, parents can become active in the education of their children and act to make changes in the school and the community around them. Educators must work with parents and students as a team. Communication and commitment are essential.

By striving to establish a democratic classroom, teachers are opening doors for students to make decisions, share experiences and knowledge, view learning as meaningful and real, and become active and global participants in the community and world. Further, when democratic ideals initiated in schools are transferred into society, dialogue is achieved, global tolerance is raised, and action is taken by empowered individuals on the promises of our pluralistic society. Through collaboration and networking with peers, administrators, parents, and community members, empowered teachers have the potential to be effective forces for change.

Many teachers are beginning to realize the importance of autonomy, networking, decision making, empowerment, and democratic education. Through teacher education programs, collaboration, and dialogue, educators must continue to strengthen their vision of democratic teaching and make their voices heard. We have a long way to go, but the journey will certainly be exciting and worthwhile, and perhaps transformative— personally and socially.

REFERENCES

Arendt, H. (1958). *The human condition*. Chicago: University of Chicago Press.

Bellah, R. N., Madsen, R., Sullivan, W. M., Swidler, A., & Tipton, S. M. (1985). *Habits of the heart: Individualism and commitment in American life*. Berkeley: University of California Press.

Bellah, R. N., Madsen, R., Sullivan, W. M., Swidler, A., & Tipton, S. M. (1991). *The good society*. New York: Alfred A. Knopf.

Beyer, L. E. (1989). *Critical reflection and the culture of schooling: Empowering teachers*. Victoria: Deakin University Press.

Beyer, L. E. (1991a). Teacher education, reflective inquiry, and moral action. In B. R. Tabachnick and K. M. Zeichner (Eds.), *Issues and practices in inquiry-oriented teacher education* (pp. 113-129). London: Falmer Press.

Beyer, L. E. (1991b). Schooling, moral commitment, and the preparation of teachers. *Journal of Teacher Education, 42*(3), 201-210.

Beyer, L. E. (1993). Communication, power, and emancipation: A contextual view of educational administration. *Journal of Management Systems, 5*(2), 16-31.

Giroux, H. A. (1989). Rethinking education reform in the age of George Bush. *Phi Delta Kappan, 70*(9), 728-730.

Goodlad, J. (1984). *A place called school*. New York: McGraw-Hill.

Goodman, J. (1992). *Elementary schooling for critical democracy*. Albany: State University of New York Press.

Greene, M. (1988). *The dialectic of freedom*. New York: Teachers College Press.

Hoffman, N. (1981). *Woman's "true" profession: Voices from the history of teaching*. Old Westbury, NY: Feminist Press.

Kozol, J. (1991). *Savage inequalities: Children in America's schools*. New York: Crown Publishers.

Maeroff, G. I. (1988). A blueprint for empowering teachers. *Phi Delta Kappan, 69*(7), 472-477.

Paulson, P. R., & Paulson, F. L. (1991). *Portfolios: Stories of knowing*. Paper presented at the annual meeting of the Claremont Reading Association, Claremont, CA.

Rubin, L. J., & Borgers, S. B. (1991, September). The changing family: Implications for education. *Principal, 71*(1), 11-13.

Wood, G. H. (1988). Democracy and the curriculum. In L. E. Beyer and M. W. Apple (Eds.), *The curriculum: Problems, politics, and possibilities* (pp. 166-187). Albany: State University of New York Press.

SEVEN

To Give My Students Wings

Katie Poduska

Imagine a small town nestled in the hills of rural Iowa. "Mt. Vernon! One hill of a town!" A town proud of its scholastic and athletic achievements: at least one National Merit Scholar each year; State 2A Football Champions. A place with middle-class values and middle-class problems. This is the environment in which I live and work, the setting in which I struggle to teach democratically.

"Mrs. P., can you help us? There are no directions on our group page and we can't figure out what to do."

"Do the best you can. Work together to figure it out. Life doesn't come with directions."

Neither does teaching. This fact, which empowers me as a teacher, has caused the most frustration in the classroom and has alienated me from my peers.

I am constantly bombarded by "experts" in all capacities who have answers for me; yet, frequently, I am not even asking the questions for which they provide "expert" answers! The push to raise test scores and to "bring back the basics" only focuses on the "what" and "how" of education. Where is the "why" in such emphases? Without looking at the why, it is impossible to evoke change, or to know if change is necessary.

How often are the true experts, the teachers themselves, consulted about the changes needed in education? If my experience is any indication, such consultation is rare. Instead, as a teacher in the public school system, I am often considered part of the education problem. Rather than being someone who needs a cure, I perceive myself as an agent of change, a catalyst for new thinking in my students and in myself. That I change as my students change is an incontrovertible fact, and says much about what I think teaching essentially is.

The process of growth is a delicate balance between affirming, encouraging, and challenging students beyond their self-perceived limits. This is not a linear progression nor is it well defined and predictable. It is often guesswork—"intuition"—on my part whether a student needs to be told "You're doing fine. Let's go on to something else" or "Try this again. You can do it!" Much of my agonizing and self-recrimination come from questions I continually ask myself:

"Am I really reaching this child?"
"How much more is he capable of understanding?"
"Will she ever realize that I am helping her cope with challenges she will face in the future rather than thinking: 'Why won't Mrs. P. help me?'"

The answers to the problems in education deal with empowerment, consciousness, and awareness as developed through democratic teaching. This is a personal journey for the teacher and the students—one that is constantly evolving and growing, often surprising and never predictable. This chapter is a chronicle of my journey: successes, failures, questions, and challenges.

To understand my journey, several questions must be answered:

What does it mean to teach democratically?
Why do I teach that way?
How do I go about it?

Interwoven throughout my answers will be some of the obstacles to teaching democratically.

WHAT IS DEMOCRATIC TEACHING?

Democratic teaching involves three components:

1. discovering and nurturing voice
2. developing consciousness
3. claiming a new awareness

These are "textbook" phrases outlining a highly exhilarating yet challenging method of teaching. In practice, the incorporation of democratic teaching involves a total commitment and an ever-demanding focus. It requires dedication to an ideal when such dedication is often in conflict with the very structure of the present educational system, and an ideal that can cause conflicts or, at least, misunderstandings among peers. It is often lonely, since a democratic vision means going beyond mastering established curricula to a wider scope involving self, others, and personal responsibility—uncharted territory in the present system.

My understanding of what democratic teaching really is has been continually evolving. How I view voice, consciousness, and awareness today is very different from my understanding of eight years ago. Voice initially meant a freeing of the inner child, a tearing away of all those obstacles that push children into decisions they do not choose. I meant to help my students rebel as I was rebelling from my own school experiences. I had the naive belief that children would be able to see the innate goodness or evil of decisions and act accordingly, with only slight direction from me. I understood consciousness as being aware of more than one possibility and awareness as acting on consciousness. This was a "natural" progression that I was eager to initiate.

I have since learned that democratic teaching is not so simple as I thought, nor is it as complicated as my peers make it out to be. I was encountering children who, in one or more areas, needed direction and guidance in developing values acceptable for our classroom. Some lacked the self-discipline to complete assignments, some were unable to get along with their peers, others had parents who cared little about them. Developing voice became a delicate issue in which I have had to continually question the values, both spoken and unspoken, operating in my classroom. Voice, as I understand it today, is the careful balancing of personal, parental, and social values through which a child is able to build a foundation for valuing different ways of thinking, living, and acting. Consciousness became more than just exposure to other ways of thinking and living. When viewed from the foundation of one's voice, such possibilities hold value: some as desirable and some not. Such judgments needed my guidance and were not "innately" discernible by my students.

Consciousness-raising is not "natural" to my students. I have often felt the need to provoke this consciousness by forcing situations on my students. An example is our M&M/world oil consumption activity (Iowa Department of Education, n.d.). The students are divided up according to the world's population: 1 person in Australia, 2 people in South America, 3 people in Africa, 3 people in Europe, 1 person in North America, and 14 people in Asia. M&Ms, representing yearly oil consumption by each continent, are distributed: 3 to Australia, 8 to South America, 8 to Africa, 24 to Europe, 39 to North America, and 18 to Asia. The students are then allowed to eat the M&Ms. What continually surprises me about this activity is how often the students fail to realize the hidden message. Many constantly talk about my unfairness to them, refusing to think about the real-world message simulated for them. The student in North America realizes her power in holding most of the "oil" but she often uses it as a bargaining tool to further her own interests rather than seeing it as an opportunity to correct inequalities. From this activity and others I have realized that awareness is a deliberate personal decision called from a consciousness-raising experience. I had envisioned myself as a challenger and a changer for my students. I now know that I am a provider of experiences and a guide to other acceptable possibilities. Change is the student's response.

Although my vision of democratic teaching has been altered over time, it is the only way I can teach. I have found my own vision of personal growth inexorably tied to the vision I have for my students. Democratic teaching is not something I do; it is something I am.

WHY I TEACH DEMOCRATICALLY: A MOSAIC OF LEARNING

"A teacher cannot call forth from her students that which she has denied in herself. She will not be able to recognize in others that which she is not allowed to claim in herself" (Poduska, 1987, p. 7).

I am a "student of teaching" (Dewey, 1904) just as the children in my classroom are students of learning. In this context, the most important question that can be asked is "why?" Such a question represents a need to discover the essence of a particular subject, the meaning and significance of our actions and theories. This is the true motive for learning. To call this forth from my students, I must also experience such a need. My why does not stop with intensive research into a particular subject. My why takes the products of the mental activity of my students and searches for connections to a larger community outside of the classroom. My why enables me to provide glimpses of other possibilities for my students so that they themselves can build their own visions. When I focus on the why of each activity that happens in my classroom, whether planned or unplanned, I am free from the limited vision of an established curriculum. What remains is a set of experiences carefully crafted by my students and me in which each of us identifies our own personal struggle. The curriculum then becomes a mosaic in which we all have an equal part, claiming ownership and celebrating its beauty. The curriculum is no longer a road map outlining a journey that I lead, while my students follow, providing interpretations of events along the way.

Building a mosaic of learning is much more difficult than following a road map. Unlike road maps, mosaics have no specific beginning or ending points. Mosaics can be constructed simultaneously in many directions at the same time by more than one builder. Road maps need only one leader and many followers traveling in only one direction. Mosaics often demand consensus, road maps compliance. From the very beginning, I decided that my classroom must become a mosaic and that such a vision meant that I would teach democratically.

To build a mosaic of learning, to teach democratically, meant that I had to establish a basic standard from which all my decisions would stem—a choice indicative of the basic focus in my classroom. I had to choose between "making the children . . . fit the system or helping the children to remake the system to fit them" (Wood, 1984, p. 220). I had to reclaim for my students a vision of the good society. But in doing so, I knew that I was faced with a paradox, so aptly described by George Wood (1984), that "the school exists to provide legitimacy for the existing social order but such legitimacy may not be possible if teachers work to meet the needs of the children" (p. 219).

This paradox is one that I think about continually as I weave my constantly changing curricula: Is the learning in my classroom supporting the dignity, worth, and autonomy of each individual or is it part of some external standard imposed on me and my students? This external standard is seen in our school's requirement to take the Iowa Test of Basic Skills each November. One week of the year is spent in the antithesis of what I believe democratic teaching to be. My students are forced to become timed producers who color in circles for answers to questions that hold little meaning for them. Why must my students deal with frustration and anxiety in school when we could be exploring the wonders of learning? Resolving the paradox described by Wood (1984) means developing strong philosophical roots. Those roots support a very tender plant—the democratic classroom—that is easily trod on by external forces: other teachers, established curricula, state-enforced standards, and even the conditioned responses of the students themselves. It is imperative that teachers guiding the growth of a democratic classroom understand as clearly as they can the basis for their decisions so that they can transform any external force threatening their philosophy into an opportunity for their children.

I become aware that my philosophy is being threatened when I feel an uneasiness about an event or activity that I think may undermine democratic values. I then begin to question and challenge the legitimacy of my students' participation in such an event. When I have no choice and must allow their participation, I transform that event by turning the reality of imposed choices into opportunities for empowerment for me and my students. I remember best a situation from several years ago. A high school student representing the Iowa Dairy Council as Iowa Dairy Queen visited our school one morning and presented a challenge to all of the fourth-grade classes: collect as many Real seals as possible to win a treat—ice cream for the whole class! The other three classes would receive yogurt. When I returned to my class after lunch, students were grabbing milk cartons from each other, frantically cutting seals from the boxes. I was disturbed because several value statements were implied: Ice cream is more valued than yogurt, one class is superior to the others, competition is more important than cooperation. I also felt that there was an undue amount of advertising propaganda being "fed" to my students. I took my concerns to my principal, who immediately stopped the contest. Fortunately, the other fourth-grade teachers also supported this decision. My next step was to involve my students in the activity I had undertaken with the principal. We held a class meeting and I asked them for their opinions about the ice cream challenge. Without my prompting, they voiced the same concerns that I had, being especially upset that ice cream was considered more of a prize than yogurt. Because of their interest and their concern about this incident, I mentioned the possibility of studying advertising: its explicit and implicit messages, gimmicks, and persuasions. Because we had just experienced a "real" advertising situation, the students were eager to explore this subject. We became critical viewers and consumers, finding many examples and opportunities to discuss the influence of advertising and the power each of us has in either legitimizing or challenging such influence. This was one of my "successes," one experience in which I could see my students claiming a new vision and becoming empowered.

It is tempting to rely on prepackaged, manufactured curriculum units that involve technically preparing the teacher for their use in the classroom. The teacher is "trained" rather than educated in the implementation. One of my most exhilarating weeks of teaching involved such a unit—programmable Lego machines. It was the "perfect" unit. Each child progresses at his or her own pace, at his or her own level, with his or her choice of projects—truly individualized learning. But as I sat back and evaluated the experience, I had my doubts. Where was the challenge and growth for my students? If students have been denied choice and have always had everything clearly delineated for them then, yes, I can see the challenge and subsequent growth in being allowed some autonomy. But if students are frequently allowed to choose, as I try to establish in my classroom, it seems to me that they tend to choose "safe" projects that they know hold few surprises for them. What should have happened with the programmable Legos is for me to have been gently urging, and perhaps prodding my students to risk new challenges. Growth does not come without change and change, at least in the classroom, is not evoked without challenge. I had ignored such opportunities, concentrating instead on what they had accomplished—a much easier task. I have learned that easy teaching is not always the most productive teaching for either myself or my students.

HOW I TEACH DEMOCRATICALLY:
A CURRICULUM OF "CANS"

I cannot decide for my students what they cannot learn. I refuse to accept a stratification and distribution of knowledge that causes ability grouping. Ability grouping means social reproduction in order to maintain the status quo in our society. It means focusing on what a child cannot learn as the deciding factor in what he or she can learn. I have discovered that "cannots" in education have become much more powerful than "cans." When I decide that a child cannot understand, manipulate, or attempt a particular activity for whatever reason, I am closing a door for that child. Implicit in such a denial is that the child is either not capable or not motivated. Only the child himself or herself can decide that. Most devastating of all is that I am developing a mode of consciousness for the child in which he or she has no decision and which will most likely be incorporated into his or her self-image. I am limiting the child's vision of possibility. There is little growth and virtually no empowerment.

Teaching then becomes for me an experimentation in "cans." I constantly ask myself, "How far can we go? What can we do next?" To view curriculum in this way is exciting for me and my students but it is not without struggle. Defining a curriculum by what could be possible rather than by what is not possible is difficult. Often the most opposition comes from the students themselves. They are used to having limitations placed on them either through group placement, usually in reading, or the implicit understanding that a particular subject is studied in another grade. My first few months of teaching each year involve breaking such imposed boundaries by giving continual reassurance: "Don't give up. Keep trying. You'll surprise yourself. Let's see what you can do."

What has surprised me most about this vision of curriculum is that while I am affirming my students, I am also reassuring myself. When I see the struggles that my students are experiencing—the frustrations and, sometimes, even tears—I constantly ask myself whether I am too subjective and demanding in my method. But my years of teaching experience have proven to me that my students will not grow if they are not challenged to change and that such a process is often painful. It sometimes takes half of the school year for my students to claim a realization of the tremendous progress they have made and continue to make.

To help my students claim ownership in this growth, I have found that frequent and caring communication is essential. Our weekly class journal in which the students dictate to me what is to be recorded is a chronology of successes and failures, struggles and triumphs. When we re-read sections previously written, students often comment on how much more they are able to do now than they were able to do at that particular time. This journal also establishes us as a "family," celebrating shared, common experiences. The recounting of these experiences brings responses such as "I remember that!" and "Can you read some more?" Reminiscing in this way has built a strong sense of community for all of us in providing linkages that cannot be made through traditional teacher-student relationships.

Daily private journals give each student the opportunity to write anything to me, without restrictions. It is in these individual journals that I become familiar with my students as persons in their own right, giving me insight into the best ways to guide them to their full potential.

Class meetings provide a sounding board for any concerns I or my students may have. The circular arrangement of desks and the opportunity for anyone, including me, to speak on any classroom subject give all of us a chance to free our voices. Playground concerns, lunchroom policies, and discipline problems have been some of the topics raised. We do not always solve our problems, but most of the students' written comments convey that the chance to express their feelings is valuable.

Claiming Consciousness

The why of learning and a curriculum of cans lead to the most important belief in my philosophy of teaching: Each child must claim a voice for expressing his or her own consciousness. This belief is my focus for teaching and protects my perspective from becoming ingrown and self-protecting. It challenges me to continual evaluation and analysis of my choices for our classroom life. The way I view my role in helping each child to claim a voice of consciousness is the essence of my dedication to democratic teaching.

Each child in my classroom has a unique voice. This voice is more than just a writing style or a relationship with peers. It is a complex expression of values expressed through interests, hopes, fears, questions, and refusals. It includes sharing with others the thoughts and visions that guide one's thinking and one's choices. It has little to do with academic performance and everything to do with response to life. Public schools, as they presently exist, do their best to mold these voices in predetermined ways. Students are labeled gifted, disabled, attention-deficit-disordered, and so forth, and this labeling becomes their voice, often without their choice. It is my greatest satisfaction and my greatest challenge to strip away such labeling

and discover the true voice of a child. Students often rebel at such
unveilings, especially those who have always perceived the "disabled" student as unable to solve any challenge. In my classroom I deliberately manu-
facture situations in which such disabled students excel so that a new
awareness of each individual's capabilities begins. It is not difficult to find
such freeing activities. Looking beyond traditional paper-and-pencil assignments and textbook activities, I have found a wealth of material incorporating logical thinking and spatial activities that do not rely on printed
words: Tangrams, pentominoes, and solid geometrical constructions are
some examples. When faced with such non-traditional tasks, disabled students have an advantage since they have had to develop strategies to cope
with daily challenges and they easily apply such strategies to non-traditional
challenges. Students who excel in traditional classrooms are often at a loss
and, to my delight, I have found them asking disabled students for help.
The results are exhilarating. Each student begins to perceive the other students differently and "groups" disappear. When the teacher no longer
labels, the students find labels unimportant and though differences are still
apparent, they are no longer considered either obstacles or advantages.
They just exist.

Freeing Voices

When I first began teaching in the classroom six years ago, I assumed
that activities aimed at freeing voices and claiming consciousness were only
pertinent to my students' lives. That assumption became a hindrance when
I found myself bound by a system that rewarded sameness and penalized
creativity and individuality. I knew that traditional teaching with traditional
methods would not effect change; it furthers the status quo. The status
quo, as I continue to see it to this day, denies children and teachers the
freedom of true expression.

It became essential to me that I begin the process of freeing my own
voice. Claiming my voice involved a highly critical analysis of content and
subject areas based on my own need to be creative and innovative. I dis-
carded my textbooks. They are someone else's voice, not mine. I needed
a curriculum of possibilities, not boundaries.

I began to question all the expected classroom activities: tests, ability
grouping, conforming to an absolute standard, searching for the single correct answer. All of these indicated a curriculum looking for sameness, not
individuality. My belief that a child must not be molded to fit an objective
curriculum became stronger as I gradually rejected each of these barriers.

Claiming my voice meant teaching holistically, weaving all subjects
together with "real-world" meaning for my students. When I tried to teach

in the traditional fragmented way with little integration, my vision was obscured. Teaching became pedantic, boring, and uninspired.

After I began to claim my own voice, I became aware of a new consciousness. I became convinced that my teaching, to be truly democratic, must be connected to a context larger than the classroom. Rather than concentrating on the mastery of specific skills in the curriculum, for example, math facts, I focused on the application of such skills—what meaning and place they have in the real world. I attempted to bring genuineness to my teaching so that my students could begin to connect with the world outside themselves. This focus on the real world has led us to "adopt" grandparents at the local nursing home, to improve our community by cleaning out the local pond during Earth Week, and to build international relations with Scottish pen pals.

I discovered that the everyday life of the classroom is rich with such possibilities. Playground conflicts are an excellent way to connect with world conflicts. For example, during the Gulf War several years ago, the fifth-grade class in our school was very aggressive in taking over popular playground equipment without regard to other children's feelings. My simple question, "Does this remind you of anything that has been in the news lately?" caused a lively and somewhat heated discussion as my fourth graders and I compared our playground problems with the conflict in the Middle East. When I first initiated and encouraged such discussions, I also made another discovery: Connections with the outside world involve values. To discuss real-life situations means that I often must take a stand based on my own sense of right and wrong. I found that this fact carries a lot of responsibility and accountability. My students are at an age when they can easily be propagandized by someone they respect. I had to be very careful that the values I presented in the classroom were those of basic human rights, and remember that the teaching of individual choices within those human rights was the responsibility of parents, not the classroom teacher.

Claiming my voice meant that teaching was no longer a neutral choice. Voices had to be heard that were not represented in my classroom: people of all races, and those who are physically and mentally challenged. It became a moral issue with me in that I felt compelled to present, to the best of my ability, politically and culturally honest information in the light of basic human rights. This viewpoint is controversial and has put me at odds with my colleagues. A teacher who cannot see that her curriculum choices are essentially political choices cannot understand my conflict in teaching such a curriculum. It has become increasingly difficult for me to remain silent. As I continue to experience the freeing power of claiming my voice, I feel more and more compelled to have others hear that voice;

I have begun to speak out at what I consider to be "explosive" meetings: curriculum discussions.

Making such choices and implementing them in the classroom can be nearly impossible within the present educational system. I have been fortunate in that my district prides itself on supporting diverse and highly individualized teaching styles. The two principals with whom I have worked have been supportive of my efforts, allowing me to experiment with and adapt the curriculum, with few restrictions, as I feel the need to do so. My colleagues have recognized my need to teach according to my beliefs and have learned that my choices do not have to be their choices. But the teamwork and cooperation that I try to instill in my students has not been possible for me with my peers. The choice to teach democratically is one in which I must dare to be different and to forge my own path. It means looking ahead to possibilities rather than following what has been done before. It means focusing on the child rather than on mastery of specific subjects. As of this writing, I have found no one willing to share that vision with me. It is in these realizations about my school's curriculum and my peers that I feel the most frustration and isolation.

The most important aspect of claiming my voice is that I allow each child in my classroom to claim his or hers. Democratic teaching demands that each student's voice be heard. Some voices are very faint, covered under layers of labeling: low academic reports, cumulative folders, teacher's comments to peers, and parents who set limitations for their children, making sure that the teacher understands and supports these limitations. The challenge is to dig through all of these layers, allowing a slow and often hesitant growth of the student's true voice. This growth is difficult to nurture because the process is unique with each child and the teacher must be finely tuned to the subtle nuances of each voice. Sometimes that means challenging the child to discover an answer through patient Socratic questioning. It may mean asking the child to try new experiences that he or she hesitates to attempt. The difficulty is in determining when the child's voice needs a resting point—a time in which urging, questioning, and careful encouraging should cease for the moment.

There is a second issue in this careful nurturing. Some students seem to present a clear voice from the very beginning. I have had students who seem to know exactly the correct phrase, the correct behavior to make themselves "tractable" in the traditional system. Often these students tend to be the "good" ones, as labeled by other teachers and parents. They tend to be pleasers rather than thinkers. These students have learned to play the academic game well and may have sublimated their own true voice in the process.

The most difficult child to free among good students is the academically gifted. I have found these students to be the most fearful of unknown challenges and the most resistant to taking risks. The true voice of such children is often deeply buried under a pattern of reinforced responses and a need to feel comfortable. Gifted children rarely stretch their capabilities to the limit. They see no need to conquer unknown territory when it is so easy to stay where all requirements are known. Such students have difficulty in breaking their academic restraints and often perceive me as restricting their progress rather than freeing them. I often cannot answer their questions because they need to work through where they are headed.

When I came to these realizations about my students, I found it necessary to test each voice to make sure that it really belonged to the student and not to another adult. I began to search out opportunities to challenge students in original ways—tasks with more than one right answer, logical thinking problems, spatial puzzles, controversial discussions with excellent arguments on both sides. The results have often been painful for the students, who can no longer easily predict what will be expected of them.

After one such unpredictable activity, a student came up to me and said that although her mother told her that she should always trust her teacher, she could never trust me again. I was shaken by her response but I began to realize that my role as teacher had changed for her and that she was reacting to that change. I was careful not to criticize or make any judgments about her response to the activity. But I had shattered her illusion of predictability. It was then that I began to realize that part of my vision for empowerment—the right to cause change—has to have an element of uncertainty. Only a static curriculum can be certain. To truly build an atmosphere of discovery the process and, at times, the product will be unknown.

While I was learning how to free my students' voices, I began to realize that these new voices needed opportunities for empowerment. They needed avenues of expression, to experiment and to test their authenticity. As these authentic voices began to emerge and became more confident, it was imperative that they begin to make decisions. These decisions had to hold meaning for my students and not be a mere token of my benevolence. My students needed to have the freedom to choose and the freedom to criticize, without any externally imposed ramifications. These criticisms had to be taken seriously with the view of effecting change. The why had to be asked and answered constantly.

I have wondered if allowing my students to make decisions would lessen my own decision-making ability, but this has not happened. It seems, at least in my classes, that allowing students to decide "awakens" them. It is apparent in their reactions. A new awareness comes on them and they treat such freedom seriously. Simple questions such as "Is this a valuable activity? Why?" help them in controlling their circumstances. The activity then becomes more than just my idea. The students themselves have a vested interest. Decision making seems to be the pivotal point when I evaluate and assess whether I am teaching democratically. The freedom to choose or not to choose, to criticize and effect change, is part of that decision making. The questions I ask myself deal with the amount of decision making I should allow my students and in which contexts these decisions should be made—questions I ask myself continually.

These beliefs were challenged when I was confronted with a child who did not want to participate in what I considered a high-interest integrated learning activity: our paper airplane unit in reading. She came up to me after the second day and said, "What if I don't want to do this any more?" My first reaction was typical: anger. I had never had a child refuse to participate in this activity before. How dare she choose not to choose something I worked so hard to make interesting and challenging for her? But I also realized that not to choose is a legitimate choice and that if I were truly teaching democratically, I had to honor such a choice. After contacting the parents to let them know of their child's decision, I decided to allow the child her choice—with one provision. Since this activity was a group project with the whole class participating, her choice not to participate meant that she chose not to be part of the class. She would then have to leave the classroom and read books on her own during the time we worked on our paper airplanes. I gave the parents and child time to discuss the options so that all would understand what this decision would mean. I was not a participant in this discussion other than outlining the possibilities from which to choose. The next day I asked for her decision. She chose to remain with the class but I was prepared to follow through with the alternative. As I began to analyze this situation, I determined that her desire to quit stemmed from frustration in making a difficult paper airplane. She was testing me to see how much decision making was really possible in my classroom. I learned from this experience that choices by my students must be treated seriously. I must be prepared to deal with student choices in ways that allow them to grow in harmony with personal and social values, building the delicate balance that is the basis for decision making.

Allowing students decision-making ability does not sever them from my role as teacher. I have found that it builds new bridges between their understanding and my capacity to trust that understanding. Empowering my students is often as simple as allowing them to openly critique an activity or assignment. I have made student evaluation an integral part of the assessment of any new activity I introduce. The students write comments to me concerning what they liked and what they disliked about the activity, what could be changed, and whether the activity should be repeated for next year's class. The most important part of their assessments for me is their answers to the why of each statement they make. To explain their reasons to me is often very difficult for them. The traditional system does not deal with why in either justification or in explanation. But in nearly every situation, I have found my students to be utterly honest and to be no more critical of any activity than I have been myself. This aspect of empowerment I value highly. How can one grow if one cannot discern that which keeps one from growing?

EMPOWERMENT AND CONSCIOUSNESS-RAISING

The greatest hindrance to a child's voice is the objective goals of a specified curriculum, which demand adherence and allow little deviation. In such a teaching situation, the child's voice is molded to a prescribed form. Students quickly learn to stifle creativity, questioning, and thinking and become remote receptacles for knowledge. A curriculum that allows each to express his or her own voice is fluid, surprising, and has elements of serendipity. But the curriculum should also provide for decision-making experiences and chances for empowerment, the act of using one's voice to effect change. Empowerment is the inevitable product of the freedom to make decisions.

Class meetings, my first attempt to build student empowerment, have proved to also develop a sense of community and family in our classroom. My efforts to set aside the hierarchical structure have added an indefinable element of trust and honesty to the classroom atmosphere. These meetings have also become a "real-life" experience for me in that I have had to justify my decisions for the welfare of the class. A recent example illustrates this. I had been using computer time as a reward for completing assignments and as an incentive for all to work more quickly. As is often the case with this tactic, relatively few students were able to earn computer time and these students were able to use the computer frequently. At a class meeting, many students objected to this practice, calling it unfair and biased. I asked for a show of hands of students who felt that way. All raised their hands, except the students who had been able to use the computers. The majority demanded that I change my rationale for computer usage and they were very willing to guide me into change. My rationale for allocating computer time was not based on the practice I had been working to establish in the classroom, and the students perceived this very clearly. My students were rightly challenging me—a most unsettling experience. But I also witnessed student empowerment in a most forceful way. I had to admit my error in judgment and establish a new criterion. I had been challenged to change by the very process I worked so hard to instill in my students; I was the beneficiary of their teaching.

Each time I encourage empowerment in my students I free myself from my own restraints and misconceptions. Just how much and how far should this empowerment reach? For years, ever since I began classroom teaching, I have decided which written assignments in the students' assignment folders should be group projects and which should be done individually. Recently I began evaluating this procedure and discovered another opportunity to give my students some decision-making experience. After I explained the week's assignments, we held a class meeting. We discussed the benefits and problems resulting in student decision-making concerning assignments. Their comments, both positive and negative, mirrored my thoughts. Their seriousness about this decision-making opportunity showed me their willingness to accept more responsibility. The result was an overwhelming desire on my part to allow each group of students (desks are in threes) to decide which pages should be done by the group and which should be done individually. A work contract was drafted by each group and handed in to me. I was amazed at the diversity of contracts. I had assumed that everyone would work together on every sheet. Only one group out of eight chose that option. The other seven groups chose a varied mixture of group and individual work. At the end of the week, all students were asked to evaluate this procedure. Nearly all felt comfortable with such decision making and looked forward to making such choices again. Although I felt such an experience was positive and supported my vision for teaching, I was unsure of my next step. Should this be the procedure for assignments for the rest of the year? How will I know each student's progress in an extended group-work situation? I still do not have answers for these questions. Perhaps I need to liberate my own notions of evaluation and invent new possibilities for myself.

To be empowered in order to cause change, it is necessary to be aware of the deficiencies of the present and to have at least a glimpse of what could be. To be fully empowered, students must be connected with the outside world and learn how to use their voices in becoming active participants beyond the classroom. The why in the classroom needs to lead to the why in the world.

Literature and Life Experience

It is for these reasons that I began incorporating consciousness-raising activities as part of classroom experience. I looked for opportunities to extend my students' perceptions into other possibilities. As I began to develop my reading curriculum after discarding the basal, I looked for materials that contained controversial subjects, would lead to challenging experiences, and would expose my students to literature they would probably not choose on their own. Two novels fitting these criteria were *Margaret's Moves* by Bernice Rabe (1987), which details the everyday life of a girl born with spina bifida and who is confined to a wheelchair; and *The Defenders* by Ann McGovern (1987), which recounts the lives of three Native American chiefs— Osceola, Tecumseh, and Cochise. These novels also provided opportunities for voices to be heard that were rarely represented in our classroom: physically challenged persons and Native Americans.

To prepare my students for the experience of becoming aware of others' life experiences, I set up reading activities according to my vision of democratic teaching. It was important to me to eliminate ability grouping and to allow each student the opportunity to claim ownership of the reading process. A "safe" environment had to be established in which opinions and reactions to literature could be valued and shared with respect. Some literature had to become a shared experience that we could celebrate as a community. To accomplish these aims, I provided parameters: Three to four novels would be offered each month, several of which were required reading for all students at some time during the school year. They would participate in group discussions, complete a student record with writing activities, and produce a final project. Students would choose which novel they would like to read, and based on their choice, they would become part of a group. To remove reading difficulties, I recorded all novels on cassette tape so that the entire group could listen and read along at the same time. Group discussions focused on analysis and evaluation, giving my students opportunities to be critical readers. My questioning was based on enabling my students to make connections between their experiences and each author's presentation: "Are these characters believable? How are they real to you? Have you ever experienced a situation like this?" Along with group discussions, I tried to bring activities into our reading that provided some insight into the character's difficulties. For example, while reading *Margaret's Moves* (Rabe, 1987), each student was required to spend a day in a wheelchair, coping with maneuvering around the classroom, using the bathroom, and going to lunch in the cafeteria. After the wheelchair day was over, a page was filled out analyzing the experience. When all in the group had had their wheelchair day, we discussed the problems of having a handicap and how others in our school reacted to the handicap. Most students seem to gain a new understanding of handicaps and see the seriousness beyond what they first considered a "fun" experience. The main character in the book, Margaret, also has an unusual talent: the ability to balance several objects on her head while moving around in the wheelchair. We mimicked this experience by balancing one copy of the novel while moving the length of the classroom. This seemingly simple activity is very difficult, and raises the student's respect for others' accomplishments when faced with unusual difficulties. Such shared experiences led to discussions about people in our school who experience different kinds of difficulties and concerns about the best ways to help them become valued people in our school.

The Defenders (McGovern, 1987) has provided a different context for consciousness-raising. Because this book presents a true picture of both the white settlers and the Native Americans concerning land ownership, the students are faced, often for the first time, with an issue in which both sides possess some element of right and some element of injustice. The three Native American chiefs are presented as persons with often conflicting values and visions, driven to choices because of the time in which they lived. As we read these stories, we discuss stereotyping, how culture influences one's view of the world, and basic human values. Before reading this book, most students feel that Native Americans are "just like everyone else," but these students have little understanding of the difficulties Native Americans have faced with the white man's drive to "settle" this continent. The messages in this book and our group discussions have become so powerful in helping my students connect with a culture different from theirs that when they read that Osceola died in prison at age 38 without rescuing his people, there is sometimes stunned silence and sometimes tears from my students as they carefully take off their headphones. Many of our discussions center on the justification for the violence recounted in the book, with students often vacillating from one side to the other, but usually heavily in favor of the Native Americans. One student admitted in group discussion, after reading about the repeated violations of peace treaties by whites, that he was "ashamed to be a white." One of the most interesting and somewhat dismaying discussions for me involved the question of whether the students and I are responsible for what happened in the past in our relations with Native Americans. Most students felt it was not their problem. They could not see that we have inherited the triumphs and failures of our ancestors. My attempts to convince them that we need to rectify such wrongs were not accepted. I learned again that the process of consciousness-raising and subsequent awareness is an individual response, one that cannot be imposed.

Unpredictability and Empowerment

Most consciousness-raising activities are deliberately planned and guided by me. Others just "happen." One such incident occurred during my first year of teaching. I had developed what I considered a simple nutrition challenge for a health unit. My aim was to see if my students could find a cooperative way to solve a group problem. Each group of three students was given a bag with plastic food. The assignment was to present a balanced meal representing all four food groups. To make it more difficult and to force the issue of cooperation, I put items from only two of the four food groups in each bag. Students were told to "do whatever is necessary to complete the assignment." I had no idea that my simple directive was actually a lighted fuse that would cause an explosive reaction. I watched in amazement and concern at my students' reenactment of all too typical attempts to deal with inequities. Hoarding, stealing, physical violence, and refusal to attempt the task were my students' solutions. I did not know what to do with these responses. As I saw the activity continue to deteriorate, I stopped it and saw that my students needed some way to express their strong feelings. They wrote comments to me and we discussed the activity as a class. This did alleviate part of the hostility, but for some students, the classroom wasn't the safe, predictable haven they had always known. My role as teacher changed from that of provider of information to that of a person giving them uncomfortable "real" challenges with the expectation that they should meet those challenges. They had become aware that we, as a class, had made some connections with some very basic conditions and that making such connections is an unsettling experience for all. I began to see growth in the consciousness of those who accepted these challenges and wrestled with them. This growth was reflected from then on in the maturity of their comments during group discussions, their willingness to work out difficult problems in getting along with others, and their ability to accomplish tasks beyond their own expectations.

I nurtured the "uncomfortableness" of such experiences as the balanced-meal activity and actively searched for others. I saw that such activities could lead to growth and change in me and in my students. But my observations of students' responses also made me realize that to allow such situations to build one's consciousness is a personal choice, one that can be made only by each individual student. A raised consciousness cannot be forced; I can only offer opportunities and hope that my students will make them their own.

I began to lead my students into probing the why of everything that came into our classroom. As I start each new school year, I instigate this questioning as part of our classroom from the first day. Although I have used other consciousness-raising activities throughout my teaching, the balanced-meal activity has been the most provocative experience I have ever initiated. I have never been able to predict how each year's class will react. Only one class over the years was able to solve the problem cooperatively; others have been even more violent in their reactions than the first class to which the activity was introduced. Each year has presented me with new insights into the culture we live in and the way our children assimilate that culture. Each year I learn again how to be a democratic teacher for the students in my care.

All of the incidents and ideas mentioned in this chapter so far have dealt with the seriousness of democratic teaching in order to lead my students to mature and responsible decision making. While building my vision of a democratic classroom, I have discovered that adding an element of fun can entice my students into becoming willing participants in many types of activities that seem to them dry and pedantic—for example, practicing math facts and spelling through games. I found myself, when I first began teaching in the classroom, judging most activities by the amount of enjoyment my students would have in doing such activities. I was responding to my students' reactions of whether they liked an activity or not, rather than focusing on the worth of such experiences. I wrestled with this concept for some time before concluding that I would, whenever possible, balance my approach to learning with both serious and not-so-serious activities. I decided that the element of fun was as necessary to the unpredictable quality of my teaching as was my focus on consciousness-raising activities. "Fun" has allowed me to use things such as food in unusual ways to help my students build concepts about our world: earthquake cake to illustrate fault movement and chocolate chip cookie mining to demonstrate strip mining. It has led me to develop units that are contemporary yet meaningful to my students—our robotics unit, for example. But I am ever mindful that to be constantly concerned about the attractiveness of a particular activity is to close my mind to other possibilities for growth in me and in my students.

METAMORPHOSIS

The process of teaching democratically is best described through the metaphor of the mealworm beetle, which we study extensively in our classroom. My students, at the beginning of the year, are much like the adult mealworm beetle. All have an exoskeleton grown through five or more years of schooling. All have accepted labeling as gifted, average, learning-disabled, and so forth, according to an external standard. All have an understanding of a system that demands conformity rather than individuality. As I begin to crack these exoskeletons by eliminating labeling, allowing some choices, and challenging thinking, larvae emerge that are anxious to feed on every experience I can offer. Feeding these larvae is the most exhilarating and rewarding part of my teaching. It challenges my own ability to meet these demands: providing common ground for shared experiences, yet weighing the validity and appropriateness of activities and making connections beyond the classroom. As the year progresses, many larvae go through a resting time, a cocoon stage, in which all they have learned becomes internalized. I know that this stage has been completed when I see my students emerge with "wings" of self-confidence, ready to tackle any and all challenges. They have outgrown what I can give them at this stage of life and are ready for new possibilities. I have often worried that my non-traditional approach will result in clipped wings when the children become part of a more traditional classroom and that they may again be forced to bear an exoskeleton not of their choosing. But I have hope that the process I am teaching—the ability to think through obstacles—will always help them to see other choices. I have hope that the experiences I have guided them through will give them insights in causing change in themselves and society—a true metamorphosis.

My greatest concern for myself is that I will become stagnant, that I will begin to build my own exoskeleton by becoming too comfortable in my teaching. If I am truly teaching democratically, there must be an element of "uncomfortableness" for me, too. I need to keep alive the feeling that "the best" is just a little beyond my present grasp. This is an aim not for perfection but for a clearer understanding of the essence of teaching. It means opening one's philosophy and subsequent decisions to criticism by peers, parents, and students—not rejecting such criticisms, but continually searching for the element of truth that can enhance my understanding of teaching. It means making connections beyond myself, becoming part of a community of teachers who strive for the same ideals and vision.

It is three days before the school year ends. A cocoon that was brought to school in the fall by one of my students shows signs of life. As we all gather around in wonder, a butterfly emerges. I look at the enrapt faces, seeing many more signs of new life. I take the butterfly to the window and place it on my hand, encouraging it to fly. It clings tightly to my finger and I return it to its container. My students say, "Mrs. P., why can't you teach fifth grade? We want you next year . . . "

It is the final day of the school year. Five more minutes and the year will be over. I take the butterfly to the window again. This time it leaps from my hand and flutters away to some new destination. Excitedly, I turn to tell my students. "The busses are here!" comes booming from the intercom. Happily, noisily, without a backward glance, my students leave the room, talking about their plans for the summer and next year—fluttering in their own way to some new destinations of their own. I am excited for them about the prospects of those destinations. I am both satisfied and saddened by the fact that during our year together we have each shed a part of our own cocoons.

I hope always to give my students wings of possibility while I remain a larva, learning what it means to be a democratic teacher.

REFERENCES

Dewey, J. (1904). The relation of theory to practice in education. In C. A. McMurry (Ed.), *The third yearbook of the National Society for the Scientific Study of Education, part I, The relation of theory to practice in the education of teachers* (pp. 9–30). Chicago: University of Chicago Press.

Iowa Department of Education. (n.d.). *Energy conservation activities for elementary grades.* Des Moines: Iowa Department of Education.

McGovern, A. (1987). *The defenders.* New York: Scholastic.

Poduska, K. (1987). A Deweyan critique of *Social studies for children*, by J. U. Michaelis. Unpublished paper for Education 312, Cornell College.

Rabe, B. (1987). *Margaret's moves.* New York: Scholastic.

Wood, G. H. (1984). Schooling in a democracy: Transformation or reproduction? *Educational Theory, 34*(3), 219–239.

EIGHT

Vision, Vitality, and Values: Advocating the Democratic Classroom

Mary Cunat

I lay on the snow at the top of "the hill," looking up at a white sky and listening to shouts and laughter from my students as they enjoyed the snow. The sense of satisfaction I felt was almost exquisite. The children were really having fun together: smiling, pulling each other on sleds, running to the top. The moment was hard-earned; we had waited for the temperature to rise enough to prevent another administrative no to our request for a White Picnic. For three consecutive days, the parent-approved event had been canceled because of subzero weather. In some ways I found myself relieved that our school administrator was authoritative when she decided against our outing. I really didn't want to risk frostbitten fingers or toes. The whole experience, however, gave me a sense of having to comply with the powers that be. More importantly, it provided students an awareness of their own lack of voice when it conflicts with those in authority. They struggled after the third cancellation, not just with accepting that their snow play was being postponed again, but with the frustrating reality that there was nothing I as a teacher or they as students could do or say to change the situation. They argued, they coaxed, and they begged, but the answer was no. They implored me, "Why don't you take us anyway? You have our parents' permission. We all have warm enough clothes." Along with my own concerns about safety, I told them I wanted my teaching contract to be renewed next year. "After all," I responded, "I love teaching here." As the answer came out of my mouth I realized that the dynamics of this experience were central to the possibilities of rebuilding democracy through education.

In this chapter I present a comprehensive view of what I think classroom teaching entails, interspersed with stories from my own classroom experiences. Within this context I hope to address some of the issues involved in developing democratic teaching practices, the difficulties and struggles a classroom teacher faces, and a number of ways I have worked to implement democratic principles in my day-to-day teaching experiences.

THE CONTOURS OF DEMOCRATIC EDUCATION

Never doubt that a small group of individals can change the world.
In fact, nothing else has ever changed the world.
                                                    —Margaret Mead

Democracy is both an ideal and a process that shapes and influences human endeavors. It is not fundamentally a system of government or a political platform, but it can influence how those systems function, perhaps especially at the micro level. Democracy is a dynamic that occurs between and among individuals and groups who are working together to effect systemic changes. At the level of a microcosm, the word *democracy* is often used rhetorically or as a slogan—perhaps in campaign promises of equity and freedom by members of political parties. It is possible that some politicians are sincerely invested in democracy, but I cannot believe that the dynamic I conceptualize with this term can be valued and/or appreciated in a political system where those in power lack authentic connections to those further down the hierarchical ladder. True democracy, as a dynamic process, is incompatible with large-scale hierarchy, where loss of individual autonomy and an inequitable distribution of resources—both material and political—are apparent.

In a large-scale hierarchy, the only way to effect social and political change is with "more power" and/or money and resources to lobby for the cause, whatever it may be. My vision of how democracy can affect a large-scale hierarchy is based in grass-roots movements—smaller groups uniting to form a larger voice. These "movements" include the "power" of many individuals, especially perhaps teachers, to influence the communities in which they work and live.

Aubrey, my five-year-old daughter, once asked me why some people speak two languages. "Because they have come here from another country, or from a family that came from another country," I replied. I mentioned friends of ours who had immigrated here, including her babysitter from Cuba. "Why do they come here, Mommy?" I explained, "Some people come here because they believe they'll have a better chance to live for themselves and their families, others because they believe they will be more free here than where they are from." "Are they more free, mommy?"

What a question. Economic injustice, poverty, social and political restraints, having to "fit in," and educational inequalities proliferate. Yet this nation still offers something special—the promise of democracy. I always get excited about this "American Experiment" when we work on the Revolution and U.S. Constitution units in my fifth-grade classroom. By the time we get to these units, students have been confronted with the ravages experienced by Native Americans at the hands of the explorers and colonizers; they know that the colonies all thrived on the slave trade and ownership of human beings; they have learned that only adult, white, male landowners had any say in political and communal decisions, and they know the status of women and children in 18th-century America. In spite of all this, a vision of democracy sparks and takes flame. We discuss the courage and integrity of a relatively small group of people to challenge and usurp the power and authority of the strongest nation in the world. The Declaration of Independence and the Preamble to the Constitution add flesh to the vision that individuals, empowered by the freedoms guaranteed in the Bill of Rights, can make a vital contribution to their community and society. Democracy is the opportunity to work at those ideals of freedom, justice for all, equality for and among all people. The individual's price for this freedom is the responsibility to maintain and build families, communities, and a society based on the principles of democracy. It is a moral imperative in a free society to work toward these goals from one's conscience and one's consciousness of one's own freedom. Moral development in children would encourage: an awareness and tolerance of individual differences; opportunities for and experiences of autonomy; critical and reflective thinking about issues regarding power, society, relationships, and rules; freedom to make choices and reflectively experience the consequences of those choices; and respect of the rights and privileges of others for all of the above. Within this context, children begin to perceive their own role as influencing and being influenced by those around them, and develop both a sense of responsibility to others and a positive sense of their own individuality. Democracy is that dynamic operating within and among individuals, who, through helping establish and acting on individual freedoms and responsibilities, are empowered to have an impact on the systems in which they live and work—changing such systems when they are at odds with the values and ideals that must undergird a democratic and socially just way of life.

As a teacher, I have come to value democracy as a real and dynamic principle in my life. When I first began teaching, in 1985, I wondered if all the reflection and theory in which I had been involved as an undergraduate would have any practical use, especially when I was faced with 30 students who barely seemed to care, much less value, what I had to offer them as an educator. There seemed to be a split between what was possible in theory and what was realistic in the classroom. At this point in my teaching career, however, I'm glad I didn't sell myself or my students short by resorting to "practical," technical teaching from the text and "managing" student behavior. I am energized by democratic teaching practices. I am challenged and excited by the process in which I am engaged day-by-day with my students. There are times I feel burned out, defeated, and fed up, but overall the rewards of being a democratic educator far outweigh the difficulties.

What is democratic education? My working definition has come to mean the vital and dynamic process of a learning community that recognizes and validates the individuality and responsibility of each participant. The community works cooperatively and reflectively to engage in experiences that are determined by aims and objectives set at the local level. Education is integrated with social development and social conscience: a sense that individuals can have a reflective and dynamic impact on the society around them and that individuals carry a responsibility to effect necessary social and political change. The overall purpose of democratic education is to engage individuals in a process that will help them develop the skills and attitudes necessary to become people who can and will contribute to the making of a vital, equitable, and humane society.

Considering this definition, I think there are a number of principles integral to democratic education. Valuing the responsibility and autonomy of each individual is fundamental. Democratic education must work to practice the ideals it embodies. Form must match content. The teaching of democratic ideals and values means little if done from a pedagogical stance that is not based on respect for the autonomy of individuals. Respect for individual choices, opinions, processes, and expression must be integrated within overall school structures and specific classroom activities. In this way the very act of teaching should carry lessons about democracy. Many times I have screamed at a class to be quiet and listen, thus escalating the noise level and losing my own sense of balance. The tone, volume, and frequency of a teacher's voice reflect in part where the power is in a classroom. Who does the talking and when? When we recognize students' rights to speak and to have their expressions taken seriously, we respect their autonomy and responsibility and assist in the development of democracy. This includes providing input into rules, procedures, and, when possible, school and classroom policies.

It is fairly common for teachers and students to "cooperatively" establish classroom rules, rewards, and consequences. This provides a semblance of student "ownership" and of reflection on rules and behavior standards. Yet there is often a hidden agenda within discussions of this type, namely, to assert the necessity or normalcy of rules whose validity is not an open question: "We all need to hear what's being said so we all have to raise our hand and be called on to speak." The difficulty is figuring out a way to function with the principle that everyone has an equal right to speak and be heard without setting up the need for hierarchical control or management. The same can be said about all "standard" classroom rules and procedures: desk arrangements, bathroom privileges, school schedules. I've personally found these to be the "crazy makers," where I am right up against the tension between being "secure" (my class is quiet and following the school rules) and being democratic (allowing students a sense of responsibility and participation). I want to help students reflect on the expectations embedded in the culture of schooling that could be creating these tensions.

An example of this is our school rule about silence in the hallways. The students understand the reason for this: "not to disturb other rooms." However, because they are a group of lively 10-year-olds, we are frequently bumping into power struggles. I feel the pressure of not "offending" my colleagues. I want to look like I have my class under "control," although I detest the implication of that phrase. There are three flights of stairs to quietly climb up and down. I have found there is only one truly honest and democratic way I can handle this: by engaging my students in reflective dialogue about the rules. We discuss the value of following rules for the sake of appearances. I present my own difficulty with the situation. We think about our responsibility to the community. We critique and evaluate my efforts as their teacher to bribe and/or coerce them into being quiet. We reflect on the personal responsibility of each individual in relation to me, their teacher, a relationship that most of them come to value. We reflect on the problems they will face should they decide not to respect this particular rule. Even though I cannot change the rule or my own personal discomfort, the students have a vital experience of reflection and evaluation. We are faced with such political and moral issues every time we trudge up and down those stairs. Students' feelings and ideas are listened to and acknowledged. They may choose to protest the rule, and consequences are again a matter of discussion, reflection, and evaluation.

There is a pedagogical idea out there that it is "effective" to ignore minor misbehaviors and cue students non-verbally to follow directions. Supposedly, verbally rewarding students who are following directions is a way to maximize desired behavior. Although I can utilize this strategy to quiet my class down, there is always an eventual clash with a few students somewhere along the line. I've come to understand that these "misbehaving" students are really a gift to show where the power struggles should and do occur. We can get students to be quiet, nicely or by threat. We can even get them to accept why they have to be quiet: "Because we need to be considerate of others (or else!)." But helping them understand all the underlying issues connected with a simple rule can be the way for them to understand more about the system, its pressures, demands, and power structures, and their own individual relations and choices in it. This is why the simple task of walking down the hall is a challenge to democratic education. What about the students who don't follow the rules? What about the children who are so determined to fit in and please the teacher that they never even question the rules? Democratic teaching principles address both of those situations in ways that respect the individual and raise questions of responsibility to the community.

In a democratic classroom students are engaged in the cooperative, reflective, and dynamic process of developing and evaluating rules and procedures. They must be permitted to critique classroom routines and activities. Recognizing and discussing underlying issues within situations where conflict arises between students and any authority figure or structural constraint is part of democratic teaching. Developing a critical attitude toward school activities gives students an opportunity to experience and express their own voice and wrestle with their voicelessness. Democratic teaching principles also include a sharing of pedagogical power. What is being taught, when it is taught, how long is spent on activities, how activities are evaluated, and who does the teaching are all areas that can be worked through from a democratic perspective.

In my school there are definite curricular goals and objectives for each subject area. I recognize that many of these goals are based on the textbook series, and I feel constrained to meet them. Often, though, I put the "content" of the goal to my class and we discuss how to go about achieving it. A recent example of this occurred in social studies when we needed to cover the main events, concepts, and people associated with the American Revolution. We brainstormed possibilities. I told them things I'd done in the past. They thought of things they'd done. We discussed suggestions from textbooks. We remembered movies about the Revolution. Eventually the students decided to do a "living history," which included narrations and skits that they wrote. Events from the French and Indian War through the Declaration of Independence were covered. My job as teacher was to help them outline significant events and generate ideas on how to best "act them out." The students were experiencing history as cause and effect and as a series of interrelated events. For instance, we imposed a classroom "Stamp Act" covering paper. We drew parallels between George III and the principal, who they felt had not been listening to their reasonable responses to having their White Picnic postponed. The students were seeing parallels between history lessons and life.

This of course takes a little more work and a lot of faith that students will be responsible for their own learning. I could test them to "make sure" they learn the concepts. Security. This reflects my need for them to be accountable so I can give the grade, "validating" the experience and "proving" that it was "effective." But it's their experience. It can stand on its own without my stamp. The real validation is in their sense of personal accomplishment. In the course of the whole human event that constituted the social studies activities, students did much more than engage with the curricular material at hand. They had a share in planning, implementing, and evaluating an entire project. They worked together, listened to each other, generated ideas, produced an exciting play, evaluated what does and doesn't get an idea across to an audience, shared power and decision making, and enjoyed maximum participation from each individual. Allowing students the opportunity to choose how something is learned is very dynamic. Even when they cannot choose the content, they can have an influence on the form, and thus reshape that content. This choosing is one principle of democratic teaching.

There are two other important democratic teaching principles that deserve elaboration. One is that every student must have equitable access to educational rewards and benefits, including resources, information, and materials necessary for learning. The second is that students must have the opportunity to process and evaluate their own personal goals and decisions and how they as individuals have contributed to the group or community.

Equitable access is a tough issue. The idea of the "haves" and the "have nots" becomes very clear in regard to classroom life when there are high and low reading and math groups, enrichment opportunities, pull-out programs, and remedial classes. We as educators are constantly trying, for the most part with good intentions, to adjust to the learning styles and levels of achievement of the individual students in our rooms. A hidden agenda becomes clear, however, when those who get the "goodies" are those who follow the rules and excel at adapting to the standards of the system. Failure to meet the standard is seen as defiance, laziness, or defectiveness in the individual, not as bias in the standards or inequities in the system that imposes them. "Fair" adjustments are made: lower reading groups, behavior-disordered and/or learning-disabled classrooms. It is not easy to determine what fair democratic practices would entail in this regard. The one thing I know I can do and have done is to be a reflective, challenging voice with my students, and as a member of the faculty. What are we really about? What is most fair? Why don't these students "fit in?" From where do our standards come?

Providing students the opportunity to reflect and share who they are, their personal goals, their own values, and their sense of self is an equally important principle. As they see themselves in relation to others, and gain a sense of how they can and do affect the people around them, a context for "power" from a democratic perspective can be set. Having students determine their own goals, and clarify their own values, is revitalizing both personally and socially. I think this kind of reflection is an important part of day-to-day democratic education. Why do we make the choices we make? Why do we work with some people and not others? For what part of an event am I responsible? What is happening in conflict situations? What is my commitment to the group? These are some of the questions students must ask themselves. I live and breathe this kind of reflective activity with my students. It is a very empowering habit. It helps me keep clear about what I'm about as a teacher, and it empowers students.

There are a number of reasons why democratic teaching is often seen as "ineffective," "too idealistic," or "too much work." I think these objections can be grouped into three major categories: systemic difficulties; the attitudes of teachers, students, and parents; and dehumanizing pedagogical language and theory.

IMPEDIMENTS TO DEMOCRATIC EDUCATION

You knew the job was dangerous when you took it, Fred.
—Super Chicken

The daily realities of teaching are rigorous and complex. Curricular demands, institutional idiosyncrasies, competition, standardization, the pressure to act as a "professional," the redundant and often meaningless paperwork, and the endless "non-curricular" but nevertheless essential daily tasks of teaching (e.g., collecting lunch money, assisting with fund raisers, filling out attendance sheets, and organizing school play rehearsals) make an ideal like democracy seem impractical and unattainable. It might be amusing to list all the little odds and ends teachers have to do during the day, but the cumulative list would not be funny. And on top of this we are expected to teach and "manage" classroom behavior at the same time! In Catholic schools such as the one I taught in for several years (which forms the context for most of the classroom descriptions included in this chapter), teachers also have mandatory uniform dress codes to enforce; public address prayers and pledges; worship services to prepare for and attend. Truly, the list seems endless.

The School System and Culture

Classroom teachers typically plug along through the day, hoping only to cover the "basics" or the core curriculum in reading, writing, and math. We are an interrupted breed. Phone calls, flu bugs, chicken pox, and faculty meetings dot the week, and if there is any time for reflection it is usually just enough to remember what one forgot to do that day. I am constantly feeling these very real pressures, which are only the beginning. I find that to attain any level of success, something is usually eliminated from my schedule. Given institutional realities, teacher reflection and evaluation may be the first things to go, since no one checks to see if they are being done. Thinking about teaching isn't a requirement for the job. Reflecting on it is sometimes even scorned.

Established curricular demands alone require more time than exists in a school day. I teach in a self-contained classroom, all subjects at my grade level. There are written objectives for each subject, largely determined by the content of the textbook. There are also system guidelines detailing how many minutes should be spent per subject per week. In the Chicago Archdiocese, for example, this includes 200 minutes per week for math, 60 minutes for art, 300 minutes for reading, and so on. Lesson planning, implementation, correcting, and evaluating take a tremendous amount of time and energy, even if one pursues the easiest possible route of plowing through the text, doing the lessons as written page by page.

My democratic values coexist with my personal need for success within the system. In my weakest year pedagogically I began my yearly planning by dividing each text into quarters, quarters into weeks, and weeks into days. I spent much of the year frustrated. Although I was "covering" the required curriculum, I had no real sense of accomplishment. The students and I proceeded from one text to the next, subject to subject, page to page. Behavior problems escalated, and I became more entrenched in trying to control everything. As a result of this and other experiences, I have come to understand that I am subject to, and sometimes internalize, the same pressure to "succeed" that affects students. Meet the criteria set forth by someone who doesn't even know you exist, and prove you did your job by checking it off from the "objectives" list, or if you're a student, shading in the appropriate circle with a number-2 pencil on an achieve--ment test.

I realized in that nightmarish year that I was evaluating myself as teacher by whether I could check off those set curricular objectives. I did teach them, after all. I still have a tendency to want to think and teach this way, validate who I am as a teacher by where I am in the text. It feels safe and solid, even if the text makes no sense and has no relevance for the students.

Security. For me, one of the biggest impediments to democratic teaching is a safe, known, "commonsense" form of security. Often the sense of security costs the very life blood of those it is supposed to protect. Often there is no proven "effectiveness," pedagogical or otherwise, to a more established format. It just seems easier to rely on familiar patterns that provide a sense of security than to take risks. To empower students and teachers with the process of choosing curricular content and form pushes on many boundaries and assumptions. It might be unsafe.

I know myself to be a teacher invested, theoretically and practically, in reflective and democratic activities. But I often take the more convenient route: using prepackaged materials and scripted teacher manuals, following stated "guidelines." The complexities, demands, and frustrations of being a classroom teacher are frequently overwhelming. Planning to do the next page in the text is so much less work and takes so much less energy, and there is little risk to me professionally. There is also little risk in coercing students to behave "appropriately"; it's always safe to dress "professionally"; it's wonderful to work diligently at improving standardized test scores. But do not take chances in allowing students to question authority. Don't go against the trends. Don't make waves. Democracy in the classroom could be dangerous.

The issues surrounding the formal curriculum are numerous. Who determines what is to be taught, when, and how? Having been on and even chaired numerous curriculum committees, I think I should have some answers for how that occurs in my school. Unfortunately, at the local level it always seems to boil down to what is easiest, most convenient, and looks best on paper. Textbooks are chosen, and the written objectives are established by the scope and sequence provided by the textbook series.

Until recently. Somehow, the message finally got through that we as a faculty could determine what and how we want to teach in the area of religious education. This occurred partly due to the leadership of a very dynamic priest who was consulting closely with me as curriculum chair. We had four very general guidelines, determined by the U.S. Bishopric. These focused on the areas of the Catholic Message, community, worship, and service. I led an in-service session primarily for reflection and brainstorming about what the individuals on our faculty wanted under the general topics. Further steps were taken to get input from parents. Administratively the idea was to refrain from giving parents "too much" space for input because that could complicate things. Asking for student input was not even a consideration. Nevertheless, the progress in giving teachers the responsibility to set their own objectives, inviting parents to express their ideas and concerns, and then choosing a text that would be closest to what was desired was a big step in a more democratic direction. I hope to see more and more of this kind of reflection on the part of the faculty as the current curriculum is revised and evaluated. I was aware of a tremendous amount of satisfaction and vision on the part of my colleagues. I can only attribute this to the fact that teachers were given an opportunity to reflect, share, brainstorm, and contribute to a very meaningful process, participating democratically in planning and developing curriculum.

A complaint I hear frequently about teaching is that there is more and more to teach and less time to teach it in. That is why the choice of what and how to teach is so vital. I've tried so many times as a classroom teacher to "fit" it all in, to the detriment of my own sanity and the real education of my students. Pressure, pressure, pressure. We always have those standardized achievement tests telling us whether we did our "real" job, and telling our students where they rank on a national percentile. We want the scores to reflect success, but so often the efforts and energy we put out for success at this level benefit only a few, and predominantly those who will test well anyway. I experience this as I watch my class struggle during test week, and I want to scream at their confusion, "But I taught that concept in October!" Then the results are out and my students' scores are compared with each other's, with their scores from last year, with those of other classes in the school, with other schools in our division, and with that national average. Somehow everyone says you aren't supposed to teach to the test. "You don't teach subjects, you teach students" is a pleasant little humanizing phrase thrown around at self-esteem workshops. But the pressure to perform is there and it is constant. The idea is that if we teach this curriculum, achieve these goals, witness improved test scores, then we will have successfully educated our students. This leaves very little space or time for democratic principles as I have come to understand them. Although I can't make the tests or the pressure to perform go away, I can participate in active and meaningful reflection and evaluation of their presumed value. That is what I offer my students and my colleagues as testing time approaches, during testing time, and when the results are in and everyone is in the frenzy of validation and comparing. I often feel very alone at this time of the year.

There are also "non-academic" but still important subjects like values, self-esteem, health, drug-abuse prevention and sex education, multicultural awareness, global education, and environmental issues we must teach. All of these topics have been added to the core curriculum, which used to include only gym, music, and art as "extras." Classroom life is becoming even more intense as schools bravely deal with the issues facing children and society today. These issues include violence, poverty, homelessness, child abuse, drug abuse, sexual abuse, alcoholism, family dysfunctionality, gangbanging, peer pressure, addictive disorders, racism, crime, pollution, injustice, unemployment, environmental destruction, and so on. All of these are very real, extremely difficult, and interrelated issues that impinge on our students' lives. I believe my school is struggling and grappling with these issues. As a democratic educator I am glad to be part of this process. But the very breadth of the demands placed on me often forces me to choose the convenient route, going for what seems the quickest and most "effective strategies," leaving me little time and energy to reflect.

Teacher, Student, and Parent Attitudes

There is a certain fearfulness influencing teachers' daily choices that undermines democratic teaching. The message that emerges from the school culture is: "conform, perform, and be uniform." I know I feel the pressure—from our principal setting standards for teachers' shoe type and skirt lengths to wanting to have my class earn the most "quiet in the lunchroom" stickers on their incentive chart. There is a very real pressure to refrain from acting "unprofessionally." I've found that word to be used by colleagues and administrators to undermine humane and democratic practices. To be considered unprofessional is an ultimate teacher fear, although nobody stops to think about what that word actually means. It means not conforming to some form of institutional expectation. A certain amount of career security is at stake if you push the limits too far. To allow students to argue and express feelings is inappropriate and unprofessional. To trust students to set their own learning goals and pace is risky and unprofessional. I've found that the word *creative* is used as a way to say "borderline unprofessional," and *enthusiastic* usually means "Watch out. This person may be a little outlandish and therefore unprofessional." Empowering students takes down the barriers between the educator on the pedestal and the "lower ranks," and is therefore unprofessional. You may not allow students to address you by your first name or to treat them with any kind of authenticity or mutuality. Professional respect is what is given students, parents, and colleagues. Don't be a real person. Thus begins the lesson on how to be a professional: Give up all authenticity, freedom, and respect for personal and political expression. It's too risky. Don't be the rabble rouser. Don't make faculty meetings last too long by asking too many questions. The hidden agenda to conform is as rigid for teachers as it is for students.

Teacher attitudes often form an impediment to democratic teaching. The first and foremost of these attitudes falls under the pressure teachers feel to "manage" classroom and student behaviors. I feel a certain responsibility to stay "in control" at all times, to know where each of my students is and to direct and influence what each is doing. "If you don't have control of your class," the saying goes, "you are not going to be able to teach them anything." How many dozens of times does a new teacher hear, "You have to be real tough at the beginning of the year, then loosen up after being in control rather than to try to regain control after they're wild"; "They don't respect you unless you're tough"; "They need consistency"; "You have to be fair, but show them who is in charge." The clichés are numerous, but the bottom line is, "*Maintain control* of your class or you're a *failure*! The kids know it. They'll take advantage of you. Your colleagues won't respect you!"

Teachers believe they can gain this control either through coercion and threat or through the correct system and/or strategy. These management models reflect the idea that students can be molded and manipulated to achieve desirable pupil outcomes. Including them in the process is valid only if it is in keeping with the management model, just as it is when a company solicits employee feedback so as to increase job satisfaction and output. Since the system is felt to be working, no real changes in it are allowed.

For me, the management models last between 15 and 20 minutes. It all breaks down because even when I do my best to implement the "name on board, check and consequence" approach, I bump into my own inability to be consistent with the routine because I am too reflective about its effects. I also believe students learn to "play the system" in these models as a way to maintain autonomy: Sneakiness, challenges to enforce the rules 100% of the time, defiance, and withdrawal are all student responses to being "managed." The atmosphere becomes oppressive. I'm sure there are many well-meaning, optimistic, enthusiastic, positive teachers implementing a management model and having varying degrees of success. I have heard the argument that students are empowered when they know, understand, and respect the rules, and they enjoy the freedom and security of having established parameters. Yet any kind of assertive discipline and/or management style that manipulates and coerces students to follow unexamined rules goes against a democratic education. Still, managing students in this way is often labeled "effective teaching." Students are on task. Results are achieved. Why do I think of Darth Vader?

Teachers' attitudes often reflect a lack of motivation due to teachers' being overworked, underpaid, and disillusioned. There is a lack of reflection on who one is and what one is about as an educator. Teachers trudge through the year, feeling they can make very little real difference in the state of things. In addition, many teachers are concerned with their own reputation among colleagues, students, and parents. There are systemic pressures to consider, such as following organizational guidelines, teacher evaluations, professional growth and development requirements, and following local procedures and routines. There is also an amazing scarcity of resources and support for doing anything other than the absolute "essentials." Essentials are determined by the established curricular and non-curricular demands, which alone are numerous and exhausting in their effects.

A lack of faith in students' ability to engage in and be responsible for any kind of decision making also impedes democratic education. It is common to hear proposals for greater student responsibility met with the claim that "maybe the brighter children could handle it, but not the others." But every classroom has "problem" children with special needs: emotionally and/or behavior-disordered, learning-disabled, language deficient, slow, "lazy." How does one accommodate the differences? Go back to the management model, try to be nice, perpetuate the problems and the inequalities.

It's a tough job. The reality is that validating and encouraging reflection and input from every child is a lot of work. But the more a child is given an opportunity to reflect and be responsible, the more reflection and responsibility a child can handle; it multiplies on itself. At a practical level this can mean treating failure or lack of compliance with as much respect as success. It can mean reflecting with students on what is happening; paying attention to their answers; being willing to make changes and adjustments based on their suggestions; encouraging them to reflect on and share their ideas, feelings, frustrations; looking for and evaluating the expectations of the system; and clarifying values in specific situations. Do I want to know how to divide fractions? Why? How will this serve me? What will happen if I don't learn this skill? Is the outcome what I want? What about this is frustrating? What can I do to make the situation better for myself? This kind of reflective activity is very empowering.

Student attitudes and self-perceptions acquired in and outside of schools also can negatively affect efforts to teach democratically. Most children have a profound lack of experience with self-responsibility. They are used to being told what to do, when to do it, how to do it, and whether they did it right. Students are not sure what autonomy means or how self-determination in a classroom can work. It takes work and experience to develop an atmosphere of trust, respect, mutuality, reflection, and responsibility. Children experience the pressure to conform, succeed, make friends, listen to parents and teachers. There is rampant low self-esteem, apathy, fear, and anger in almost all classrooms. These emotions result not just from students' difficulties at home, but from living with school structures that deny respect, integrity, and autonomy. Children are told that "success" means achieving the behavior and academic standards of the system. When children are invited to question these standards and to reflect on who they are, what they think, and what they want, they often experience this freedom (or lack of rigidity) as chaos. This makes it difficult to teach self-responsibility. I want to maintain some sense of leadership and guidance in the classroom without basing it on power over them as the teacher. The tension is constant, and often I find the need to feel "secure" and "validated" tempting me to be in complete control. I have heard argument after argument that children want and need structure. They fall apart without it. They need security, consistency, discipline. They need to know exactly what's expected of them in order to function. This is a sneaky and pernicious myth, because it seems so quantifiable.

Democratic education is not synonymous with anarchy or chaos. It allows the students to be part of developing the structures from which they are working. They reflect on and critique the very content and form imposed on them by the system. The difficulty is motivating students to be engaged in this process in meaningful and dynamic ways, recognizing that non-compliance, defiance, and rebellion at the classroom level may sometimes be part of the picture. Sometimes we must allow students to question how best to make an impact on the system when we experience it as unjust, but this is rooted in each individual's taking an active and responsible role. Working with children to develop this attitude is vital to democratic education.

Parents above all want their children to succeed in school. They believe a good education increases opportunities for a good life. The parents I encounter are well meaning. Their ultimate goal for their children is that they become decent and successful human beings. Parents fear the failure of their children, and often will blame the system or the teacher for it. However, there is a lack of opportunity for reflection and empowerment with which parents might effect real educational change. One consequence is that parents commonly perceive the school failures of their children as a reflection on them. Parents' attitudes are an impediment to democratic education when they only want their children to passively learn what they are supposed to learn and to follow the rules.

There is a certain ease in an authoritative system that discourages reflective and democratic processes. To parents, everything looks clear on the surface: Their child did or did not break a rule, did or did not do the assignment; the teacher did not explain the math clearly; another child pressured their child to steal the money. Rules and consequences provide parents an apparently reliable sense of security about where their child stands in the system. If their child is failing, and they know it's the child's fault, they can coerce, bribe, or motivate him or her to do better. They can help him or her to succeed. If it's obviously not the child's fault, they can complain, change schools, or just wait until next year and a new teacher. There may be no channels for parents to really involve themselves in discussion, support, or reflection on the actual day-to-day events their child faces. How to participate in all this and when to find the time are questions not often asked.

I encourage parents to engage in meaningful and reflective dialogue with their children about what happens in school. I encourage parents to talk to each other and to be involved in dialogue with administrators and other teachers. There is a parent organization at our school. As far as I know its role is primarily to support and help develop a sense of school community— the members don't see themselves as a political force. This perhaps would pose a threat to the school structures already in existence. The major "discussions" on school policy for most parents take place at basketball games, fund raisers, or social events. These are "behind the scenes" complaining sessions that of course would be considered inappropriate or invalid channels of expression. There is a definite openness on the part of our school administration to hearing what parents have to say, but I wonder if there are significant opportunities to reflect on the need for changes. Even if there were, I wonder if the majority of parents have the time, energy, and motivation to get that involved. It is easier to trust our children to the "professionals" and the system. Parents feel perhaps some extra sense of involvement in a parochial school because they pay tuition and expect a humanistic, child-centered education. They have chosen to send their children to this school. Other than parent-teacher conferences, report cards, notes home, and occasional phone calls, parents pretty much let the schools and teachers educate their children without much interference, reflection, or feedback from them. There are parents who make an attempt to get involved and have a say; they perceive themselves to be advocates for their child and feel they have a right to speak and expect to be heard. It is these same parents whose very names can cause teachers' eyeballs to roll. The general attitude regarding parents who get involved in other than helping or supportive roles is that they are a hassle. There is a real need for some clarity and reflection on just what parents can and should do to contribute to a democratic educational process.

I must admit that even the thought of this makes me feel insecure, because I fear the very things I value: a sense of responsible and reasonable accountability, a sharing of power, an effort to listen to all opinions. Listening to parents' feelings and ideas about issues and expectations in school may complicate things and make teaching even harder. Then again, it may energize and revolutionize the entire educational effort. The vision of parents, teachers, students, and administrators working cooperatively to shape and develop meaningful educational processes and goals would seem quite ridiculous to most educators. It's impractical. It assumes too much responsibility and experience on the part of the many. I see no other way that the educational systems can really go, however, if we are to "revitalize democracy." Educational institutions are places where we can begin to experience this vitality, initially, just by making active reflection and participation in dialogue part of our daily practice. The impediment might be the belief, a part of the hidden agenda, that teachers, students, parents, and people in general are too busy, too tired, too lazy, too uneducated, too unmotivated, too disillusioned, to get that involved and to be that reflective.

School Language

The very language used to talk about teaching can undermine the pursuit of democratic teaching practices. *Management* is just one of the many catchwords that are becoming increasingly common in talk about teaching. *Outcomes, strategies, effectiveness, productivity, on-task, reinforcement, reprogramming, technological skills,* and so on, are labels that dehumanize the educational process. They make it seem as if the right "programming" will produce highly productive and skilled (and thus *educated*) students. If a teaching method or strategy is proven "effective" regarding a prespecified "outcome," then teachers are encouraged to utilize it. If something is quantifiable, it is even better. We can prove we are doing our jobs as educators by counting the number of minutes that 85% of our students are on-task. It's even better if they like the task. More and more pressure exists to do it all: create a positive and challenging learning environment that maximizes every learning potentiality. Within this framework, power sharing is encouraged if such "ownership" increases effectiveness, but who and when and what the power sharing or reflection entails is entirely up to the one in charge. When one is thoroughly enmeshed in all the effective and quantified strategies, any weakness or lack of success can be blamed not on the system, but on the child or the teacher. Somebody didn't get it right. No questions are asked about what "it" is and whether "it" should be done in the first place. The pressure to conform to that teaching style is pernicious. We all want to be good teachers. In the face of all these great "results" obtained by our colleagues, we sometimes forget what a good teacher is and who says so.

REFLECTIONS ON POWER AND EMPOWERMENT

The administration in the school discussed in this chapter gives individual teachers a tremendous amount of leeway to develop and implement learning experiences. Written curricular goals are established, revised, and evaluated every few years for each subject, though the means of achieving these are left to teachers to decide. I have felt a tremendous amount of freedom and support from my administrator to grow and develop along my own lines. Democratic education isn't fully promoted (yet) but it is at least not blocked at every turn. Furthermore, there are many opportunities at my school for empowering involvements, primarily on committees that really do have power to make changes and decisions about school policy and goals. At faculty meetings and in-service activities, participation is generated and there is an openness to teacher comment and reflection. There is time set aside at each meeting for discussion on specific issues that affect schools and schooling on a larger scale. I take advantage of the opportunities to work at democratizing my school. As a committee person I try to create more opportunities and challenges for reflective and responsible teaching. I appreciate the fact that I am at a school where this is possible.

As a classroom teacher, I democratize by allowing and encouraging active student reflection and participation in a variety of levels and experiences. Initially, this takes the form of discussion, evaluation, and brainstorming sessions about meaningful issues, problems, decisions, and experiences. Meaningfulness and relevance are also open to students' judgment. Not everyone has to be engaged in every discussion every time. Class activities may or may not take precedence over conflict resolution, and children are invited to work out conflicts themselves.

Shared ownership and responsibility for the classroom property, space, and environment are an important part of day-to-day life. As the year progresses, students begin to break the habit of always asking permission to use the stapler, the tape, the pencil sharpener. Respect for personal belongings is a strong value, but it is mutual between the teacher and the students. I do not look in students' desks without their permission. There is an evolving mutuality about how we treat each other. With respect to environment and space, students actively reflect on and make decisions about room arrangement. The walls are full of *their* work, not the latest prepackaged poster kits.

I am constrained as a classroom teacher to meet certain curricular goals. I am part of the faculty committee that sets those goals, so it isn't that I completely object to them. Actual instruction can become most democratic by opening these goals up to the students and by giving them leadership and guidance within a plethora of learning choices. I set the ball rolling and the students take it from there. In my classroom I use learning centers in which students choose from a variety of activities and experiences. I also encourage student-led instructional time, sharing the responsibility with students to help each other. Any "grouping" of the children is based on how they are doing with a particular skill and/or their own interests. I refuse to have high, medium, and low groups; instead I have fluid groupings. Students may move in and out of groups daily, even hourly, depending on what they and I perceive their needs to be. I utilize a theme to integrate learning units and involve students in brainstorming ways to work on the skills relevant to the theme. For instance, water was the theme one year. We integrated ideas regarding the world's oceans and major river systems, environmentalism, poverty and famine relief, scientific properties and states of matter, poems about water, measuring water, salt and fresh water habitats, percentages of water in living matter, and water as a cultural and religious symbol.

Students are motivated when they are invited to participate and develop a theme. They come in with more suggestions every day—they see what is being learned as relevant to day-to-day life. In addition to having many group projects, I also utilize many cooperative learning activities. Cooperative learning can be a dynamic part of democratic education if it is enacted in ways that empower students. It can be a reflective process that strengthens and reinforces the contribution and responsibility of every individual. Unfortunately, cooperative learning can also be subject to autocratic control and judgments. Democratically oriented cooperative learning would include students in the planning, implementation, and evaluation of various activities. It goes further than teacher-controlled and/ or outcome-specified cooperative learning. Often, regular forms of cooperative learning include an element of competition and may have implicit hierarchies. Some children are considered leaders and others followers. Teachers often form cooperative-learning groups based on their perceptions of students' abilities so that groups can effectively do the job or task set up by the teacher. Democratically based cooperative learning would permit children to question their own roles in the group experience. It would not reinforce the judgment that some children are more capable of leadership and therefore are entitled to more power in the group.

Another experience I encourage is the formation of classroom committees. These committees have the responsibility to reflect on, plan, and implement classroom activities, events, or decisions. One year we had an "art project" committee, as well as committees for bulletin boards, learning centers, conflict resolution, field trips, newsletters, chores, and responsibilities. Committee members would talk to other students before coming up with a "policy" or idea, which would then be presented to the whole group and discussed. Needless to say, discussing, arguing, and voting are frequent occurrences.

I am strongly inclined to use "hands-on" activities and learning experiences in my classroom. Textbooks become resource or reference materials with which we clarify ideas and concepts or find examples. Use of the basal reader is done in a critical and reflective way. I like to get as much participation and interaction from each student as I can. I believe that "learning by doing" allows students to check out their perceptions and experiences with others. This permits reflective and critical thinking that generates inductive reasoning and allows students to arrive at their own conclusions. What they learn, therefore, has the satisfaction of meaning something to them experientially. Hands-on learning also accommodates all learning styles, and therefore permits more equitable access to educational benefits.

I am probably most covert in my own attempts at defying traditional systems of evaluating and grading students. At my school there is a specific grading standard based on percentages. I cringe at the arguments I hear to maintain this kind of grading system. I have been called on at different times to try to "justify" a grade given in terms of the work I've corrected and students' test results. The implication is that if a teacher grades too high, educational standards are too low. Correcting and grading are constant devils on my back. My "job description" includes filling out those report cards every quarter. Again, to the credit of the administration, the format and content of the report cards are being evaluated and revised by the faculty with the purpose of creating a more meaningful assessment and reporting tool. Nevertheless, there exists in general an assumption that if everyone "succeeds" the standard becomes meaningless and we could be teaching nothing. Throw in those achievement test scores and we have a mire of semi-objective evaluations of student progress.

My efforts to incorporate democratic principles in this area have included a variety of thrusts. The first is to encourage self-evaluation as much as possible, especially on projects and activities, which make up a large portion of my classroom interactions. The second is a "no-failure" campaign on any kind of specific skill and concept work, for which a written grade is given only after students have been given every opportunity to master that skill. Objective tests are balanced with open-ended, reflective essay tests. Students evaluate their own learning on a test with key questions like "What did you find to be the most meaningful part of this unit for you? Explain your answer." Retesting to improve scores is always an option. Student-constructed quizzes and tests are part of our classroom activities. Students also evaluate, critique, and participate in grading each other's work. Peer tutoring, support, and reflection are incorporated in the evaluation of student progress. Teacher-student discussion on goals and progress toward them is also a key way to ease the difficulty of having to grade and label student achievement.

If a student just doesn't "get it," or chooses not to, reflection and discussion are encouraged. A critical look is taken at the standard, and at the relevance of the particular skill or behavior where failure is being experienced. The word *failure* itself becomes a point of reflection within the context of the system. The overall context of student evaluation, grading, and achievement becomes another challenge to incorporate democratic principles. The meaning of success and being part of a system that thrives on competition and standardization are issues we address. I hope that by our engaging in this process, the letter on a report card actually has some meaning for the student.

Perhaps the most daring way I engage in democratic education is through my efforts to create an awareness of the realities and expectations of the "system." I encourage a critical viewpoint on what students experience as teacher "control," student misbehavior, classroom procedure, academic curriculum, school policy, and schooling in general. Students are challenged to think in terms of power, and how it is played out in their lives. I disseminate information to them in order to clarify areas over which they may have very little power to effect change. We look at underlying issues where there are no choices given. We brainstorm solutions when we perceive the system to be diminishing important values. Students are allowed to challenge authority, or at least to question it, when they regard situations as unfair or undemocratic. The context for trying to develop our own political voice is balanced with the issues of fitting in, succeeding, being responsible, and reflecting honestly about our personal goals in given situations. This is a very meaningful and dynamic process, which is the crux of democratic teaching. What do I value? What do I want? What really matters? What can I contribute? How? What am I up against? Where's the power? The opportunity to reflect on these questions in a variety of contexts provides the backbone of my teaching for democracy.

Overly standardized and management-oriented teaching methodologies contribute to the demise of civic literacy in our society. A democratic society can thrive only when its citizens are informed, reflective, literate, and able to think critically. Literacy and critical thought by individuals are absolutely essential to counter and change inequalities and injustice in the system. The ultimate goal of literacy and education is to have the individuals of society capable of contributing to and developing the structures and institutions in which they participate. Literacy and critical thought can help alter current relations of power. Power within individuals can lead to political and social change. The "have nots" in the educational system primarily come from the communities in our society that already lack economic and political power: minorities, immigrants, the handicapped, and those with learning difficulties. These groups may not "test" well, they may not be as well behaved, and they may not value "fitting in." These are the very groups that especially need access to and experience with democratic education, both in form and in content.

Power has many contexts. I think empowerment of students, teachers, and parents includes reflection on how power is played out daily in our personal relationships—like those that arise in trying to schedule White Picnics and in climbing up and down stairways. When I do entertaining and interesting activities with my students, I experience a tremendous amount of personal power. This is not power *over*, but power *through*: energy, vitality, creativity, fun, and humor are all aspects of satisfying relationships. We all feel the impact of each other's differences and similarities. We value each other's views. We celebrate diversity. We acknowledge conflict and seek to understand its sources. A sense of well-being and belonging accompanies the respect and acceptance of the individual. Individuals are invested in what is happening in their lives, community, city, nation, and world, and are willing to work, share, cooperate, and change. Tolerance and reflection are balanced with justice and responsibility. Democratic education empowers the individual: It provides a political voice, a social voice, a personal voice, in accord with which students and teachers pay attention to what matters to them, to what is just and fair, to what "runs" them at times.

Sometimes insecurity runs me. I have anxiety and fear that my students, despite my best efforts, won't get what they need. I fear escalating noise levels, that what we are working on isn't making sense or doesn't have real educational value. Occasionally the pressure builds and I lose my temper, imposing all the authority invested in me by the hierarchy. Then comes the frustration and embarrassment of my having to work through with my students the aftermath of my very undemocratic use of power. This in itself becomes a dynamic and meaningful experience for all of us. My students witness an adult doing what she can to take responsibility for her own "stuff." They see in me a willingness to be vulnerable, to change, to be honest about the processes in which I am involved, and to keep working at it. There are also elements of forgiveness and acceptance adding to my sense of personal value. And there is hope. I do not want to leave out the importance of this spiritual dimension as I reflect on power and empowerment. Much of what gives me a sense of purpose is trusting the human process. This means sorting through who I am, what I do, who others are, what matters, and why.

Ultimately, the progress of the human race is at stake. I feel the weight of this as an educator in every student interaction in which I am involved. It's not just a matter of teaching curriculum democratically, but of being a vital, reflective, and empowered human being trying to model in my own daily choices the values by which I live. Joseph Campbell said "The vitality of a vital person vitalizes" (Public Media Video, 1989). This is my goal for myself as a teacher who values democracy: to allow my vision, reflection, and vitality to empower students as learners, decision makers, critical thinkers, contributors to democracy, and most importantly as vital and dynamic human beings concerned with bringing about a just and peaceful world.

Much of what makes education democratic is a willingness to engage in an open questioning process. There must be a sense of respect for all individuals' contribution to the learning community and a faith that human beings can make vital and meaningful changes for the improvement of all. Democratic teaching encompasses a willingness not just to get feedback but to share power—to make images of "success" less important than the very meaningful experiences of the students. It invites reflection on all the structures, systems, and routines in which the learning community finds itself engaged, with the purpose of creating meaningful and dynamic changes where necessary. It matches in form what is implicit in content: To form a society based on democracy, its individuals must have the skills and commitment necessary to participate in, challenge, and change the various communities in which they live and work. The growth that results ripples out. It is personal, familial, communal, and societal. That is vitality!

REFERENCE

Public Media Video. (1989). The world of Joseph Campbell, Volume 1: Transformation of myth through time: The soul of the ancients. Wilmette, IL: Author.

NINE

Conclusions:
A Look Backward and the Road Ahead

Landon E. Beyer

It would be pretentious and insulting to the reader for me to attempt to summarize the previous chapters, or to speak for the authors in this regard. Those chapters stand on their own—offering insights, reflections, perspectives, and analyses that are illuminating and powerful in their own right. What I will do here is, first, focus on what I take to be some common threads among the different frames of reference that have been presented. For despite the diversity of experiences and the varying reflections on those experiences that the authors present, there are important underlying commonalities, especially regarding what public school and university educators might do differently in the future. There are also implications for how our educational institutions might be restructured. These commonalities and implications need to be underscored. Second, I want to look particularly at the relevance of the ideas and insights presented in these chapters for the interconnections between schooling and the preparation of teachers, as we continue to work toward reforms in those areas. These insights are especially relevant for me personally, as faculty, students, and staff at Indiana University, Bloomington, work with school people to reinvigorate and rebuild teacher education—virtually "from the ground up."

TEACHERS AND COMMUNITIES

In discussing the particular context of her teaching, Katie Poduska (Chapter 7) notes the sense of isolation she often felt, especially from other teachers in her school. She speaks of a definite sense of loneliness within the school as an institution (though not in her classroom, to be sure), in part because her approach to teaching is seen as unconventional by, or is at least unfamiliar to, the rest of the teaching staff. She rightly credits the school district's policy of supporting diverse, individualized teaching activities, and clearly takes to heart the satisfactions and joys provided by her students. However, in discussing her sense of professional isolation, she notes that because her teaching has caused conflicts or misunderstandings with others, "it is often lonely since a democratic vision means going beyond mastering established curricula to a wider scope involving self, others, and personal responsibility—unchartered territory in the present system." Katie is a person with deep-seated commitments and ideals, dedicated to acting them out in her classroom, and her courage and perseverance, often in the face of indifference if not adversity, are to be admired. In many respects she exemplifies the sort of person who has made the monumental effort necessary to develop and maintain her autonomy and a sense of hope and possibility in the face of sometimes daunting forces and trends (toward deskilling, socialization into institutional norms, and the like). This is the kind of teacher autonomy, hope, and possibility to which undergraduate preparation programs should be committed, as outlined in the introduction.

Katie herself clearly recognizes the need to reach out to people with divergent views, as well as to incorporate contexts outside the classroom. In her discussion of a "mosaic of learning," for instance, she acknowledges the need to reach beyond the confines of her classroom. In part this is because teachers who are serious about asking the "why" questions regarding education and teaching must see the connections between answers to those questions and the larger social realities with which they are connected. As a "student of teaching," Katie recognizes the power ideas have not only to change her consciousness and that of her students, but to alter activities and patterns beyond the classroom door. All of the authors included in this book actively work toward creating such ideas and frequently see their power demonstrated in daily classroom life.

At the same time, a number of authors insightfully point to the need to develop cooperative relationships and networks with others—within and outside the school. Several of the authors talk about this need in terms of the metaphor of "building bridges." Noelle Hawk Jaddaoui (Chapter 5), in particular, discusses at length the bridges she built and maintained: with her own college experiences, with "regular/mainstream" teachers, with her principal, with the parents of her students, and so on. She makes clear the connectedness to other people, as well as to principles and ideas, that were crucially sustaining for the development of her approach to democratic teaching. This may be especially true during the frequently turbulent first year in the classroom. The bridges Noelle constructed provided not only support for alternatives, but a sense of community that helped sustain her. Similarly, in discussing his emphasis on cooperation and community, Erin Roche (Chapter 2) is conscious of the need for collective efforts both for himself and for his students. As a component of empowered, democratic education, these values were central to his own teaching. He wonders, for example, "what format best fosters my sharing of power and decision making with others? What sort of bridge can I make with others who differ with my views? How can the tension between my ideals and existing social constraints be resolved without compromising principles?" This building of bridges with others on behalf of creating a community was vital for Erin not only in terms of his own ability to develop his vision in the classroom, but in terms of dealing with others, especially those in positions of authority, who may have conflicting ideas. This too was a central part of our teacher education program. Even the most reflective, rigorous, committed teachers are not likely to be effective if they cannot explain and defend their perspectives to others who do not share them. This is especially the case, of course, with new teachers who have strong convictions and principles that diverge from the mainstream.

A kind of bridge construction was also evident in Joni Garlock's (Chapter 4) discussion of how the "walls" that divide people and the ways of thinking in schools injure students and teachers. In demolishing the walls that separate people and activities, including subject matters, she recognized and responded to the need for bridges across which people who are different, and ideas that are divergent, may cross and even, from time to time, co-mingle. Such bridges may build both trust and understanding, if not agreement.

This effort to form links or build bridges with others is also central to Ushma Shah's (Chapter 3) discussion of Teacher Centers. These centers could serve not only as focal points for teachers committed to collaboration, but as places where they could interact with individuals and groups from outside the schools as well. This may have special relevance for urban school districts. As Ushma says:

> If the realities of some current city school budgets do not allow for photocopying, updated texts, and other necessary resources, and if we are truly concerned about educating students in equitable ways, then Teacher Centers may provide a realistic option. In addition to providing equipment for teacher use, similar to the movement toward collaboration in teachers' lounges, Teacher Centers could expand this model of dialogue among teachers beyond the school.

As we move toward the further restructuring of schools, it is vital that we include in our efforts to create communities and build bridges to those who are not employed in schools but have a vital interest in their improvement. Consistent with the emphasis on inequality that was central to the critically oriented teacher preparation program at Knox College, bridges to the poor and disenfranchised, to people of color, single parents, and members of other marginalized groups, may be especially conducive to the search for social justice.

It is important, at the same time, that the search for community and bridge-building not lead to the sort of conformity that many of the authors describe in their schools, and in education generally. In the section of Chapter 8 with the heading "Teacher, Student, and Parent Attitudes," Mary Cunat reminds us of the sometimes numbing sense of normalization that attends classroom practice. "The message that emerges from the school culture," Mary tells us, is, "'conform, perform, and be uniform.' I know I feel the pressure . . . to refrain from acting 'unprofessionally.'" Because *unprofessional* is often a code word for practices that diverge from "the way things are," or from what has come to be accepted as "given," unprofessional actions are often precisely those that challenge the status quo. None of the authors included in this book want to assist in maintaining an uncritical allegiance to the educational or social status quo. The communities and forms of cooperation that must be built to help reinvigorate schools, and universities as well, must be aimed at reinforcing forms of critical reflection; active, diverse avenues of inquiry and analysis; and open debate and challenge. While we attempted to foster these in our college courses and programs, it is at least as important that they be sustained in a restructured culture of schooling.

CRITICAL TEACHING AND UNPREDICTABILITY

Many of the authors paint an appealing picture of openness, unpredictability, and spontaneity in day-to-day classroom life that is bounded by commitments to democratic teaching. This openness and unpredictability must be nurtured and celebrated, for those very realities are not sufficiently valued in schools. Instead, spontaneous redirection of events and an openness to student input and decision making are often dismissed as resulting from teachers' failure to have students "under control," or perhaps a result of their inadequate planning, resulting in a reduction of students' "time on task." While it is distinctly *not* the case that democratic teachers spend less time than more conventional teachers thinking about how to organize effective classroom activities, there seem to be two forces at work that account for the phenomenon of unpredictability.

First, as the authors make clear, there is a collective ownership of activities in the democratic classroom that grows out of the commitment to respect students' voices and perceptions, and to share decision-making responsibilities. When Joni Garlock (Chapter 4) initiated the mural project with her high school students, for example, she solicited ideas and involvements from the students that helped shape the final product; these could not have been neatly prefigured by a more static, imposed list of behavioral objectives. Generally, democratic classrooms are decidedly rather unquiet places, where students may pursue communal projects, discuss ideas and issues in cooperative-learning groups, suggest alternatives to the teacher and other students, explore new and interdisciplinary subject matter, and so on. The classrooms described in the preceding chapters just do often tend to be noisy, exciting, even turbulent places. As Joni summarizes this, "If a visitor were to walk into my classroom on any given day he or she might see total chaos: paint everywhere, students standing, sitting, talking, thinking." Consider again the excitement and variety of the rain forest activities undertaken in Krista Sorensen's classroom (Chapter 6). The enthusiasm for and joy of learning displayed by her fourth graders, the "ownership of knowing" she shared with them, is not conducive to the orderly, tightly controlled, quiet classroom that has been regarded as the prerequisite for successful teaching.

Second, the unpredictability of classroom events is closely related to the inherent "messiness" of democratic practices in general. A commitment to making collective decisions as members of a community, to possibility that is always "becoming," mandates the sacrifice of more "efficient," outwardly pacific, hierarchically driven mandates. As we broaden the base of participation, things get noisier, "messier," and even more confused, from time to time. As Noelle Hawk Jaddaoui (Chapter 5) puts this:

> Whenever there are group decisions to be made, the chance that disagreements will break out is great. But when students are faced with an abrupt end to a popular project about which they cannot work out their differences, complex negotiations begin to take place that are often surprising. These negotiations aren't always successful, of course. Sometimes I have to help sort out what the problems are. But sometimes I can't. The democratic process is nothing short of unpredictable.

Elementary school students, like all of us, bring with them perspectives, reference points, and past experiences that are sometimes different from those of others. Occasionally these differences lead to conflicts whose resolution cannot be neatly engineered, especially as we move away from more authoritarian modes of control. Resolutions are not pre-given, but must be worked out in practice, sometimes with few precedents and hardly ever with detailed blueprints. Democratic decision making can indeed be cumbersome, and from time to time frustrating.

Besides external constraints on teachers that work against spontaneity—for example, mandates from administrators or criticisms from other teachers—there are more subtle, cultural influences that work against the spontaneity so clearly valued in this book. For instance, the pressure to "succeed," in particular to conforming to rather static institutional definitions of success, can be a strong deterrent to initiating alternatives that are central to democratic process. Such pressures can be intense at times, even for the committed teachers whose reflections are included here. The real need to get hired and rehired, to gain approval for alternatives when they are at odds with the mainstream, and to be seen as a valued colleague can lead to an embrace of the conventional, even if only for a time; we all, occasionally, seek the "safe haven" and the security it brings. Mary Cunat (Chapter 8) eloquently cautions us about those dangers, as they dampen enthusiasm for risk-taking:

> One of the biggest impediments to democratic teaching is a safe, known, "commonsense" form of security. Often the sense of security costs the very life blood of those it is supposed to protect. Often there is no proven "effectiveness," pedagogical or otherwise, to a more established format. It just seems easier to rely on familiar patterns that provide a sense of security than to take risks. To empower students and teachers with the process of choosing curricular content and form pushes on many boundaries and assumptions. It might be unsafe.

In an environment where predictability and standardization have been seen as hallmarks of professionalism, it is especially easy to be lured by the comfortable and the commonsensical. It takes a great deal of courage, and conviction, to resist such forces. Yet the authors seem united in their view of risk-taking as fundamental to good teaching. This willingness to take risks was apparent in the work of many students as they were taking classes with me. Ushma Shah (Chapter 3) recounts her own growing critical consciousness during her undergraduate days, as she worked "with friends and campus organizations to confront and address controversial issues of 'political correctness,' student voice, and the CIA." Further, she says she became aware of "the importance of interrogating common perspectives and of challenging paradigms. Tutoring high school students and working with adults through the Heartland Literacy Coalition, I learned the power of teaching, the empowerment of teaching." This same dedication to interrogating the conventional was clear in Ushma's classroom activities at South Elementary School when, for example, she and her students worked through issues related to the beating of Rodney King, and the "selective tradition" that operated through the curriculum materials in her classroom. Taking risks and good teaching often seem synonymous.

Of course all of the teachers have experienced successes and failures, joys and disappointments, in their classrooms. Commenting on her own struggles against the pressures for safety and security, and her efforts to remain true to her ideals and principles, Mary Cunat (Chapter 8) says, "planning to do the next page in the text is so much less work and takes so much less energy, and there is little risk to me professionally. There is also little risk in coercing students to behave 'appropriately.'" Yet it is not safety and institutionally defined appropriateness that drive Mary and the others. Somehow, in spite of all the odds, against all the pressures that work toward security and safety through adopting the dominant cultural messages of schools, the teachers whose work appears here have managed to thrive. They have found ways to protect the non-linear, unpredictable, sometimes joyous qualities of unanticipated or redirected events as these transpire in the democratic classroom. No human activity of any complexity, after all, can always be tightly controlled, no real person always "on [someone else's] task." Reflecting on both the frustrations and joys of teaching, Mary reminds us:

> It's a tough job. The reality is that validating and encouraging reflection and input from every child is a lot of work. But the more a child is given an opportunity to reflect and be responsible, the more reflection and responsibility a child can handle; it multiplies on itself. At a practical level this can mean . . . reflecting with students on what is happening; paying attention to their answers; being willing to make changes and adjustments based on their suggestions; encouraging them to reflect on and share their ideas, feelings, frustrations; looking for and evaluating the expectations of the system; and clarifying values in specific situations. . . . This kind of reflective activity is very empowering.

A final cultural reality that undermines the kind of spontaneity and involvement that characterize democratic teaching is the reality of standardized testing in our schools. Interestingly, virtually every author mentions the frustration and anxiety created by these tests—as well as their incompatibility with democratic teaching. Not only do these tests fail to provide insights into classroom activities for which success cannot be reductively quantified; they create anxiety for both students and teachers. They also cast the beauty and struggle of learning as something mistakenly thought reducible to a numerical equivalent. For democratic teachers especially, standardized tests are the antithesis of genuine learning. As Katie Poduska (Chapter 7) puts this, "the push to raise test scores and to 'bring back the basics' only focuses on the 'what' and 'how' of education. Where is the 'why' in such emphases? Without looking at the 'why,' it is impossible to evoke change, or to know if change is necessary." Another example of how objectified, seemingly neutral measures are thought to predict success, standardized tests stifle autonomy and creativity, and work against the sort of critical activities to which the authors are committed. Portfolios and other kinds of more qualitative evaluations show much promise in helping us loosen the grip of standardized tests. The fourth graders in Krista Sorensen's room (Chapter 6) clearly benefited from this alternative. As Krista describes them, reflective portfolios "do not contain meaningless pieces of paper, but instead collections that indicate student learning and growth. The purpose of these portfolios is to celebrate that growth." Consistent with the orientation to teacher preparation discussed in the introduction, Krista continues by emphasizing that "reflection is the most important part of this process." Such evaluation measures allow for the spontaneous and the unpredictable while encouraging reflective understandings of learning by teachers and students.

TEACHING AND GROWING

One of the more surprising discoveries in reading the chapters of this book may be the extent to which the authors have pursued activities, courses, programs, and degrees since the conclusion of their undergraduate education. At one level, for me and others who know them, at least, this is not all that remarkable, given the authors' abilities and inclinations. Yet continued involvement in scholarly endeavors outside the classroom does speak to what I believe is a central notion in teacher education and genuine professional development. There are two aspects to this. First, for those of us working in programs that lead to initial certification, we must be honest enough to give up the illusion that at the end of four years of coursework and field experiences graduates are "teachers." Even the best, most dedicated, most thoughtful graduates require years of experience before they realize anything like their potential. Indeed, such a day may never come, since teaching is literally a lifelong process of growth. Noelle Hawk Jaddaoui (Chapter 5) notes, as do others, the stresses and strains of her first year. While these stresses may change character over time, partially as a result of new expectations, they never disappear altogether, especially for searching, creative, reflective teachers. This is part of the excitement, as well as the exhaustion, of teaching.

It is this searching, reflective attitude that I believe resulted in these authors' continuing scholarly work. Whether we consider Mary Cunat's work with other teachers and administrators on curriculum development, Katie Poduska's coursework at the University of Iowa and her plans to enter a Ph.D. program, Krista Sorensen's enrollment in a Master's degree program at National-Louis University, Noelle Hawk Jaddaoui's involvement with the Chicago Area Writing Project, the National Endowment for the Humanities grant Joni Garlock received to study at UCLA during the summer of 1995, Ushma Shah's graduate studies leading to a Master's degree from the University of Illinois at Chicago, or Erin Roche's work with Honduran teachers as part of his Peace Corps activities, each of the authors has maintained the social, moral, and political vitality, and the intellectual curiosity, that is vital for continued growth.

A more realistic assessment of the role of teacher preparation programs within the larger context of teacher development does not diminish the importance of undergraduate education. Indeed, such an assessment may make initial teacher preparation even more important. Those of us working in such programs must, given the inherent limitations of what we do, be careful to ensure that we incorporate those areas of scholarship, inquiry, and action that will have more long lasting effects. We must also recognize the lesser importance of more technical proficiencies that may be better acquired through sustained practice in the classroom. This implies that relatively less attention be paid to "how-to" questions, and more attention to larger issues and debates—to those "why" questions that many of the preceding chapters have highlighted. It also means connecting how-to questions to why questions, recognizing that theory and practice must intermingle, creating that emphasis on praxis noted specifically by Erin, Ushma, and Krista.

This leads to a second point that has critical relevance for teacher development. It remains common practice for graduates of teacher education programs to be certified, to find a position in a public school district, and then to be left alone to "sink or swim" as their own actions, and someone's evaluation of them, allow. At best, teachers may be provided short, in-service activities or workshops that deal with a particular topic or issue. Such activities do not promise the kind of active, intellectually sustaining involvement that is necessary for continued growth.

THE PROMISE OF COLLABORATION

I haven't stopped building bridges. It is possibly the single most important activity I have engaged in as a new teacher.
—Noelle Hawk Jaddaoui

I think a supportive, like-minded group of teachers, meeting on a regular, frequent basis, would have provided further strength to my reflections and actions.

—Erin Roche

Perhaps the most frequently heard contemporary buzzword in the teacher education community, "collaboration" is often seen as the next step toward wide-ranging school, and perhaps university, reform. What collaboration means, however, and how it might be maintained, is not always so clearly spelled out. Here again I think we have much to learn from the ideas presented in the chapters in this book.

Many teachers convey feelings of being rushed, of there simply not being enough time to do all that is expected of them. No doubt this is partly because working closely with 25 to 30 children for 6 or 7 hours each day just will often be emotionally draining. But there is more at work here, especially for the kind of teaching portrayed in these chapters. For these teachers are continually asking the hard questions, of themselves and others. As Mary Cunat describes her own self-examination: "What do I value? What do I want? What really matters? What can I contribute? How? What am I up against? Where's the power? The opportunity to reflect on these questions in a variety of contexts provides the backbone of my teaching for democracy." Asking and answering such questions is much more difficult if teachers are deprived of a community within which they can be discussed and if they do not have the time or energy to pursue them. The most experienced teacher included in this book, Mary reminds the reader that teachers "are an interrupted breed. Phone calls, flu bugs, chicken pox, and faculty meetings dot the week, and if there is any time for reflection it is usually just enough to remember what one forgot to do that day." Moreover, given current priorities in most schools, "teacher reflection and evaluation may be the first things to go, since no one checks to see if they are being done. Thinking about teaching isn't a requirement for the job. Reflecting on it is sometimes even scorned." Erin Roche, the most recent college graduate, expresses similar concerns about how time is spent in schools:

> Mundane teaching tasks and the need to comply with external forces devour my time for praxis. It is hard for me to think about gender issues or personal empowerment as I'm filling out daily attendance forms or setting up lab equipment. There isn't much time for my students to discuss classroom rules or fair desk arrangements when we are concentrating on covering grammar rules for their upcoming Iowa Test of Basic Skills.

The sense of always being hurried, of constantly being distracted, of running on a treadmill the speed of which is adjusted upward by someone else as we appear to be making headway, is familiar to most teachers—whether they work with second graders or college seniors. If professional development activities are to make a difference, and if collaboration is to be a real possibility, with significant effects, something must change.

One possible change that is being discussed and to some extent implemented is a closer alliance between public schools and universities. While this is an idea that has won fairly wide approval, its implementation is rather complex, in part because of the sharp cultural differences between public schools and universities. Keeping in mind the ideas and perspectives of the authors, allow me to conclude with a few comments about the possible future of teacher education and professional development.

Currently, Indiana University, Bloomington, like a number of institutions of higher education, is attempting to sponsor research projects of a collaborative sort with local schools. Our Research Institute on Teacher Education (RITE), in its second year of operation, has funded a number of collaborative inquiries with teachers at both levels. RITE has as one of its primary missions the improvement of teacher education and the enhancement of public school activities through joint research projects. Indeed, proposals are not funded that fail to include K–12 and college teachers as co-researchers. This is one promising avenue for improving both public school and college education, and of making some impact on school restructuring.

If collaborative projects such as these are to be meaningful, teachers must be provided some relief from the other duties for which they are now responsible. This is possible on only a relatively small scale through undertakings like those supported by RITE, which provides funding for released time for teacher-researchers. For the long haul, though, considering the constraints on teachers' time and the need for greater opportunities for reflection and inquiry, more must be done. The structure of the school day and year must be altered, with time allotted for the kind of reflection and interaction that are the prerequisites for teacher development. This is by itself a major economic and emotional issue, respectively, for school districts and individual teachers. Action research projects, tied more directly to classroom-based phenomena, provide a valuable possibility in this regard, for prospective and practicing teachers and university researchers alike. They may enable educators to work together to create the kind of praxis valued by the authors, making more real the forms of critical inquiry to which we are all dedicated.

Whatever we may think of the potential for more collaborative research and other relationships, however, we must be clear that collaboration "only" names a process. It does not tell us what we should do with the collaborative relations we create, nor what values ought to guide the undertakings that result. We must be sure to continue to ask the kind of critical questions the authors of this book have raised in the preceding pages, and keep in mind the political, moral, and social nature of inquiry and teaching. The portrayals contained there, though, ought to make us less pessimistic, more hopeful, than those of us in teacher education sometimes are.

Currently, as Director of Teacher Education at Indiana, I am working with members of the teacher education community (undergraduate and graduate students, university faculty and staff, and public school teachers and administrators) to revise teacher education. Meeting bi-weekly since January 1995, the Teacher Education Steering Committee created five tentative principles to guide our efforts to rethink teacher education: Critical Reflection, Development of Personal and Social Meaning, Community, Commitment to Education as a Continuous Process of Intellectual and Spiritual Growth, and Individualization and Personalization. This multiyear effort involves not "tinkering at the margins," but rethinking and reconceptualizing what teacher education means within this institutional context. That context varies dramatically, in certain respects, from the one at Knox College outlined in the introduction. The number of undergraduate teacher education students, for example, is roughly two and one-half times as large as the entire student body at Knox; and the number of professors working in the School of Education here far outstrips the total faculty at Knox.

On the other hand, it is not obvious that the values and perspectives on which the Knox program was based are not relevant to my current position, in spite of the differences in context. Just how far this will turn out to be the case remains to be seen.

In the meantime, the pride I take in the teachers who worked with me on this book, noted at the end of the introduction, has only grown as a result of the work we have done over the last—can it be?—three years. If my efforts at Indiana University bear fruit of similar quality to that represented in *Creating Democratic Classrooms: The Struggle to Integrate Theory and Practice*, we can be assured that the future "is in good hands," educationally and socially.

About the Contributors

Landon E. Beyer is Associate Professor and Director of Teacher Education at Indiana University, Bloomington. His interests include curriculum theory and development, alternative approaches to the preparation of teachers, the arts and aesthetic education, and the social foundations of education. He has published widely in scholarly journals on these and related topics. He is co-author, with Daniel P. Liston, of *Curriculum in Conflict: Social Visions, Educational Agendas, and Progressive School Reform* (Teachers College Press, 1996), and senior editor (with Michael W. Apple) of *The Curriculum: Problems, Politics, and Possibilities*, second edition (State University of New York Press, forthcoming).

Mary Cunat is currently teaching at a magnet elementary school in Chicago. The school draws top-achieving children from around the city, reflecting ethnic and socioeconomic diversity. Although an experienced teacher, she has just entered the public school system and finds many new kinds of challenges to her democratic values and beliefs. Mary is an active member of numerous environmental education organizations. She lives in Chicago and has one daughter, Aubrey.

Joni Garlock is currently teaching at Havana High School in rural Illinois. She is also a working artist with several paintings in the permanent collection of the Illinois Art Educator's Association's Electronic Gallery. Joni is also working on her Master of Fine Arts Degree at Bradley University.

Noelle Hawk Jaddaoui is entering her sixth year teaching English as a Second Language in grades K–5 at David E. Walker Elementary School in Evanston, Illinois. She has participated in the Chicago Area Writing Project and has become qualified to be a Teacher Consultant. She spends a significant amount of her personal time reading professional literature in her search for ideas that will lead to more holistic and democratic practices. One of her future ambitions is to pursue writing, possibly as an author of children's books.

Krista Sorensen received her undergraduate degree from Knox College. During her undergraduate years, she completed an Honor's project that included field work connected to the Chicago School Reforms. She anticipates completing her Master's degree in education at National-Louis University in Evanston, Illinois, during 1995–1996. Krista has taught English as a Second Language in a multiage classroom and is currently teaching second grade.

Katie Poduska is in her eighth year of teaching fourth grade in Mt. Vernon, Iowa. The mother of four children, she is working on a Master's degree in elementary education with the hope of someday earning a Ph.D.

Erin Roche was born in Elgin, Illinois. He graduated from the Illinois Mathematics and Science Academy and from Elgin College. He received a BA degree with majors in Mathematics and Elementary Education, Phi Beta Kappa, from Knox College. He has recently returned from working with Central American educators, and is now teaching bilingual students in Illinois.

Ushma Shah has been teaching in the Chicago Public Schools for the past three years. She is currently teaching in a new K–8 program entitled "Collaborative Arts." She completed her undergraduate degree at Knox College and received a Master's degree from the University of Illinois at Chicago.

Index

Ability grouping, 13, 121
Accountability
 for classroom order, 6, 37-38, 59-60
 for standardized test scores, 6, 39, 46, 69, 78-79, 95, 100, 110, 137
African-Americans, and slavery, 4
American Association of University Women, 15
American Dream, 97
American Educational Research Association, 21
American Educational Studies Association, 21
Anderson, J. D., 4, 15
Apple, M. W., 2, 6, 8-10, 16
Apprenticeship system, 5
Arendt, Hannah, 98
Ashton-Warner, Sylvia, 41, 59
Associated Colleges of the Midwest, 45
Authority. *See also* Empowerment; Power
 and rules of schools, 67-68, 81-82
 student attitudes toward, 27-28, 33-39
 and student voice, 127
 teachers and, 55-57, 68-70
Ayers, W., 19

Barber, Benjamin, 16, 74
Barone, T. E., 13
Basal series, 77-79
Bastian, A., 16
Behavior modification techniques, 6
Bellah, R. N., 2, 17, 74, 97, 102
Bennett, W., 2
Beyer, Landon E., 1-26, 3, 6, 7, 13, 14, 16, 22 n. 5, 75, 87, 98, 150-161
Bigelow, B., 53
Bilingual students, 15, 100-101, 128-129

Bloom, A., 2
Borgers, S. B., 96
Bowles, W., 10
Brown v. *Board of Education*, 4

Campbell, Joseph, 149
Carnoy, M., 17
Chicago
 Local School Councils in, 19, 58
 Urban Education Program, 15, 45-59
Chicago Area Writing Project, 77, 83, 158
Chicago Religious Task Force on Central America, 18
Child and the Curriculum, The (Dewey), 44
Civil War, 4
Classism, 44
Classroom committees, 145
Classroom management and control
 as impediment to teaching, 138-139
 and power of teachers, 59-60
 schedules in, 70, 80, 135
 student interests versus, 37-38
 teacher accountability for, 6, 37-38, 59-60
Classroom practice, of English as a Second Language (ESL) teachers, 79-85
Cohen, J., 17
Collaborative communities, 55, 57-59, 103-104, 158-161
Common schools, 5-6
Consciousness-raising, 108-109, 113-114
Cooperation, 18-19, 145
Cornett, J. W., 10
Counts, George S., 16

Cremin, L. A., 4, 32
Critical thinking, 16–19
  and literacy, 147–148
  in teacher preparation, 7–10
Cuban, L., 9
Cunat, Mary, 15, 18, 21, 127–149, 153,
  155, 156, 158, 159
Curriculum
  basal series in, 77–79
  decisions concerning, 136–137
  and deskilling of teachers, 50–51, 111–
  112
  and diversity of students, 98
  goals and objectives of, 132, 135
  hidden, 9, 88
  and limitations on teachers, 47–50
  and lists of "things to know," 50
  multicultural, 45, 48–49, 52–54, 122,
  129
  selectivity in, 9
  student interests versus, 29–30, 34, 35–
  37

Dale, R., 10
Decision making
  for curriculum, 136–137
  in democratic classrooms, 81–82, 94–
  95, 100, 118–120
  teacher role in, 102–103
De facto segregation, 4
Defenders, The (McGovern), 121, 122
Deinstitutionalization of teacher
  education, 5
De jure segregation, 4
Democracy
  definitions of, 73–74, 97–98
  nature of, 128
  participatory, 15, 30–31, 74, 82–83, 97–
  98
  representative, 2, 74
Democratic classrooms, 16–20, 27–40,
  87–104, 127–149. *See also*
  Democratic teaching
  characteristics of, 89, 130
  class meetings in, 111, 113, 120
  cooperation in, 18–19, 31–32
  creating, 89–97
  critical awareness in, 33–34
  decision making in, 81–82, 94–95, 100,
  118–120

  development of rules in, 81–82, 90–91,
  130–132
  impediments to, 35–39, 95–97
  initiating, 40, 81–85
  moral and ethical dimensions of, 32–33,
  129
  ownership in, 30–31, 88–89, 112–113,
  121, 130–132, 143
  participation in, 15, 30–31, 74, 82–83,
  97–98
  personal meaning for students in, 29–
  30, 34, 35–37, 51–54, 92–94
  requirements of, 17, 98
  sense of community in, 15, 31–32
  societal influences on, 95–97
  student attitudes toward authority in,
  27–28, 33–39
  whole-class discussions in, 67–68, 69
Democratic education
  defined, 130
  impediments to, 134–143
  nature of, 128–134
  open questioning process in, 149
Democratic teaching, 106–126
  components of, 107–109
  consciousness-raising in, 108–109, 113–
  114, 119–124
  methods for, 112–119
  new awareness in, 109, 115, 124–
  126
  reasons for, 109–112
  unpredictability in, 116–117, 122–124,
  153–157
  voice in, 108, 113–119
Densmore, K., 6
Deskilling of teachers, 5–6, 7, 19, 50–
  51
Dewey, John, 16, 21 n. 2, 22 n. 3, 44, 59,
  98, 109
Dialectic of Freedom, The (Greene), 97–
  98
Disabled students, 114, 121–122
Dramatization, 82
Dysfunctional families, 96

Educational reform
  financial aspects of, 102
  teacher role in, 54–59, 98–100
Educational society (Bellah et al.), 102
Egg-carton syndrome, 63–66

Empowerment, 87-104
 and knowledge, 88-89
 parent, 101, 148-149
 student, 27-39, 53-54, 82, 84, 91-97,
  113-119, 148-149
 teacher, 19, 34, 98-101, 104, 119, 148-
  149
English as a Second Language (ESL)
  students, 15, 75-85
 and authority relationships, 27-28
 and bureaucratic limitations, 100-101
 classroom practice with, 77-85
 democratic approach with, 81-85
 Literature Circles of, 84-85
 Writing Workshops of, 83-84
Equality of opportunity, 2, 133
Erickson, G., 13
Esland, G., 10
Evaluation
 grading in, 60, 146
 student, 60, 93-94, 95, 133-134,
  146
Everhart, R. B., 10, 19

Factory model of education, 60
Failures, educational, 146-147
Feinberg, W., 3, 9
Fernandez, Joseph, 8
Finn, C., 2
Franklin, B., 6
Freedom, 97-98
Freire, Paulo, 13, 16-18, 41, 44, 59
Fruchter, N., 16
Fuller, F., 5

Garlock, Joni, 18, 21, 62-72, 152, 154,
 158
Gifted students
 student teaching and, 45-59
 and unpredictability, 116-117
Gintis, H., 10
Giroux, Henry A., 9, 10, 16, 97, 98
Gittell, M., 16
Goodlad, John, 98
Goodman, J., 98
Good Society, The (Bellah et al.), 102
Gordon, J. A., 4
Grading systems, 60, 146
Greene, Maxine, 16, 18, 59, 97-98
Greer, C., 16

Grimmett, P., 13
Grouping, 13, 121, 145
Gutmann, Amy, 16

Haskins, K., 16
Heartland Literacy Coalition, 155
Heath, S. B., 15
Henry, J., 9
Hess, G. A., Jr., 19
Hidden agenda, 133, 138
Hidden curriculum, 9, 88
Higher education, teacher education
  versus, 3, 5
Hirsch, E. D., 2
Hoffman, Nancy, 3, 4, 99
hooks, b., 15
Houghton-Mifflin basal series, 77-79
Huebner, D., 6

Illinois Goals Assessment Plan (IGAP), 46,
 47, 95
Immigrants, and teacher education, 3
Individualism, 2, 97
Inquiry-oriented programs, 7-10
Integrative approach, 17
Intrinsic motivation, 53-54
Iowa Department of Education, 108
Iowa Test of Basic Skills, 39, 46, 95,
 110
Isolation, teacher, 19-20, 55, 57, 63-66,
 75-76, 150-151

Jackson, P. W., 9
Jaddaoui, Noelle Hawk, 6, 15, 20, 21, 73-
 86, 151-152, 154, 157, 158
Janitors, 76
Johnson, Elmore A., 85 n. 1
Journal writing
 class, 113
 student, 113
 teacher, 65

Kantrowitz, B., 8
Kaufman, P. W., 32
King, Rodney, 48-49, 156
Kliebard, H. M., 6
Knowledge
 and empowerment, 88-89, 103
 nature of, 79, 103
Kozol, Jonathan, 4, 102

Labeling, 116, 124
Lacey, C., 7
Laird, Susan, 22 n. 4
Language
  and effective learning, 96
  as impediment to education, 143
Liston, D. P., 13, 16
Literacy, and critical thinking, 147–148
Literature Circles, 84–85
Local School Councils, 19, 58
Lomotey, K., 15
Lorde, Audre, 42
Lukes, S., 2

Macdonald, M., 10
Madsen, R., 2, 17, 74, 97, 102
Maeroff, G. I., 103
Mann, Horace, 4
Mansbridge, Jane J., 16
Margaret's Moves (Rabe), 121–122
Massachusetts Board of Education, 4
Master teachers, 5
Mattingly, P., 3, 21 n. 1
McAnich, Amy, 22 n. 4
McCarthy, C., 10
McCutcheon, G., 10
McGovern, Ann, 121, 122
McKersie, W. S., 19
Mead, Margaret, 128
Meaningfulness, search for, 29–30, 34,
  35–37, 51–54, 92–94
Mentors, teachers as, 6
Meritocratic education, 1, 8
Mirel, J., 19
Mitchell, C., 10
Moral education, 3, 4–5, 13–15, 32–33,
  99, 115, 129
Motivation. *See also* Empowerment
  student, 53–54
  teacher, 139–140
Muelder, Hermann, 11
Multiculturalism
  and curriculum content, 45, 48–49, 52–
  54, 122, 129
  in New York City, 8
  teachers' experience of, 43–45

Nasaw, D., 3, 9
National Commission on Excellence in
  Education, 79

National Endowment for the Humanities,
  158
New Expressions (newsletter), 52
Newman, F., 2
New York City, multicultural curriculum
  of, 8
Normal schools, 3–4, 5, 6, 100

Objectives, pre-assigned, 47–50, 77–79,
  111–112
Observation, during student teaching, 58
Ogbu, J. U., 15
Ownership
  in democratic classrooms, 30–31, 88–
  89, 112–113, 121, 130–132, 143
  shared, 144–145

Pagano, J. A., 3
Parents
  alienation from schools, 71
  attitudes of, 141–143
  empowerment of, 101, 148–149
  relationships with teachers, 70–72, 76–
  77, 101
  in unstable and dysfunctional families,
  96
Parent-Teacher Association (PTA), 76–77
Participation, in democratic classrooms,
  15, 30–31, 74, 82–83, 97–98
Pateman, Carole, 16
Paulson, F. L., 94
Paulson, P. R., 94
Pedagogy of the Oppressed (Freire), 44
Poduska, Katie, 19, 21, 106–126, 109,
  150–151, 157, 158
Poppleton, P., 5
Portfolios, 93–94, 95, 157
Portfolios: Stories of Knowing (Paulson
  and Paulson), 94
Poverty, and teaching as moral action, 15
Power. *See also* Authority; Empowerment
  of teachers in classrooms, 59–60
  in teaching/learning communities, 57
Praxis, nature of, 38–39, 44
Principals, relationships with teachers,
  55–57, 68–70, 81, 111
Professional development activities, 157–
  158, 160
Professionalism, of teachers, 7, 138, 153
Professors of Curriculum, 21

Progressivism, 16
Public Media Video, 149
Pullin, R., 5
Purpose, and democratic classrooms, 29–30, 34, 35–37, 51–54, 92–94

Rabe, Bernice, 121–122
Racism, 44
Raskin, M., 17
Reading. *See also* Textbooks
  literature and life experience in, 120–122
  Literature Circles and, 84–85
  student choice in, 30
Reflective approach, 38–39, 44
  journal writing in, 65, 113
  portfolios in, 93–94, 95, 157
  student, 133–134
Report cards, 60, 146
Representative democracy, 2, 74
Research Institute on Teacher Education (RITE), 160
Responsibility, shared, 144–145
Rethinking Schools, 18
Rich, A., 13
Roche, Erin, 15, 19, 21, 27–40, 28, 152, 158, 159
Rogers, J., 17
Ross, E. W., 10
Rubin, L. J., 96
Rugg, Harold, 16
Rules
  and authority, 67–68
  in democratic classrooms, 81–82, 90–91, 130–132
Rumberger, R., 17

Sarason, Seymour B., 1
Schedules, 70, 80, 135
Schön, Donald, 13
School districts, 77
  and bilingual programs, 100–101
  and diverse teaching styles, 116
Schooling
  assumptions concerning, 1–3
  and barriers in education, 62–72
  as force for economic and cultural reproduction, 9–10
  hierarchy in, 54–57, 88, 89, 99–100
  meritocracy in, 1, 8

moral development and, 3, 4–5, 13–15, 32–33, 99, 129
  as progressive force, 16
  and society, 95–97
School secretaries, 76
School system
  and culture, 135–137
  as impediment to democratic education, 135–138
  students versus, 66–68
  teachers versus, 68–70
Sears, J. T., 10
Secretaries, school, 76
Security, as impediment to democratic education, 136
Selznick, P., 17
Sexism, 44
Sexual abuse, 18, 70–71
Shah, Ushma, 6, 13, 18, 21, 41–61, 44–45, 152–153, 155–156
Shannon, P., 2
Shearer, D., 17
Simmons, A., 40 n. 1
Sirotnik, K. A., 9
Slavery, 4
Sleeter, C. E., 15
Smyth, J., 13
Socialization process, in teaching, 6–7
Sorensen, Krista, 15, 19, 21, 87–105, 154, 157, 158
Standardized test scores, teacher accountability for, 6, 39, 46, 69, 78–79, 95, 100, 110, 137
Stanley, W. B., 16
State educational goals, 69
Strom, Bruce, 22 n. 4
Student-centered learning, 53–54
Students
  attitudes and self-perceptions of, 140–141
  attitude toward authority, 27–28, 33–39
  and barriers in education, 63–68
  bilingual, 15, 100–101, 128–129
  in development of rules and procedures, 81–82, 90–91, 130–132
  disabled, 114, 121–122
  empowerment of, 27–39, 53–54, 82, 84, 91–97, 113–119, 148–149
  English as a Second Language (ESL), 15, 27–28, 75–85, 100–101

Students (*continued*)
  evaluation of, 60, 93–94, 95, 133–134,
    146
  journal writing by, 113
  and ownership in democratic
    classrooms, 30–31, 88–89, 112–113,
    121, 130–132, 143
  teacher attitudes toward, 140
  versus the school system, 66–68
  voice of, 82, 84, 113–119, 127
Students of color, and teaching as moral
  action, 15
Sullivan, W. M., 2, 17, 74, 97, 102
Swidler, A., 2, 17, 74, 97, 102

Tabakin, G., 6
Teacher Centers, 58–59, 152–153
Teacher empowerment, 19, 34, 98–101,
  104, 119, 148–149
Teacher preparation
  critical inquiry and, 7–10
  deinstitutionalization of, 5
  and deskilling of teachers, 5–6, 7, 19,
    50–51
  as field of study, 12
  higher education versus, 3, 5
  inquiry-oriented programs of, 7–10
  mainstream approaches to, 3–7
  moral guidance and, 3, 4–5, 13–15, 32–
    33, 99, 115, 129
  normal schools in, 3–4, 5, 6, 100
  professionalism in, 7
  role in educational reform, 103
  socialization process in, 6–7
  student teaching in, 45–59
Teachers
  accountability for standardized test
    scores, 6, 39, 46, 69, 78–79, 95, 100,
    110, 137
  attitudes of, as impediment, 138–140
  and barriers in education, 63–66, 68–
    72, 138–140
  bridges formed by, 75–77, 151–153
  collaborative communities of, 55, 57–
    59, 103–104, 158–161
  and cultural issues, 43–45
  and curriculum rigidity, 47–50
  democratic approach of. *See*
    Democratic classrooms; Democratic
    teaching

encouraging dialogue among, 57–59
isolation of, 19–20, 55, 57, 63–66, 75–
  76, 150–151
master, 5
as mentors, 6
motivation of, 139–140
and praxis, 38–39
professional development of, 157–158,
  160
professionalism of, 7, 138, 153
relationships with parents, 70–72, 76–
  77, 101
relationships with principals, 55–57,
  68–70, 81, 111
role of, 2
and school reform, 54–59, 98–100
seeking advice from other, 58–59, 65,
  75–76
subject-specific focus of, 65–66
voice of, 98–99, 114–116
Teachers' unions, 58
Teaching styles. *See also* Democratic
  teaching
  diversity of, 116
  observation of, 58
  traditional, 64, 77–79
Tenner, Cindy, 46–49, 53–56
Test scores. *See* Standardized test
  scores
Textbooks
  basal series, 77–79
  critical approach to, 18, 146
  and curricular goals, 132, 135, 136
  and deskilling of teachers, 50–51
  development of, 2
  increased use of, 6
Thematic teaching, 92–94
Thompson, Jennifer, 52
Tipton, S. M., 2, 17, 74, 97, 102
Tracking, 13, 121

United Kingdom, teacher preparation
  in, 5
Unstable families, 96
Urban Education Program (Chicago), 15,
  45–59

Vallance, E., 9
Vocational/technical training, teacher
  education as, 5–6

Voice
  importance of, 20
  nature of, 108
  student, 82, 84, 113–119, 127
  teacher, 98–99, 114–116

Warren, D., 3
Weiler, K., 10
Weis, L., 8
Whitson, J. A., 3
Whole-class discussions, 67–68, 69
Williams, R., 8, 10

Willis, P., 10, 19
"Women's work," teaching as, 3–7, 99–100
Wood, George H., 16, 98, 110
World Past to Present, 52, 53
Writing
  Chicago Area Writing Project, 77, 83, 158
  journal, 65, 113
Writing Workshop, 21, 83–84, 93

Zeichner, K. M., 7, 13